Sabre & Foil

Sabre & Foil

Two Instructional Accounts on Fighting with Swords

ILLUSTRATED

Lessons in Sabre, Singlestick, Sabre & Bayonet; or,
How to Use a Cut-and-Thrust Sword
J. M. Waite

'Foil Practice' & 'Notes and Observations on the
Art of Fencing'

George Chapman

LEONAUR

Sabre & Foil
Two Instructional Accounts on Fighting with Swords
Lessons in Sabre, Singlestick, Sabre & Bayonet or, How to Use a Cut-and-Thrust Sword
by J. M. Waite
'*Foil Practice*' & '*Notes and Observations on the Art of Fencing*'
by George Chapman

ILLUSTRATED

FIRST EDITION

Leonaur is an imprint of Oakpast Ltd

Copyright in this form © 2022 Oakpast Ltd

ISBN: 978-1-915234-72-8 (hardcover)
ISBN: 978-1-915234-73-5 (softcover)

http://www.leonaur.com

Publisher's Notes

Contents

Preface

In the pages of this *Manual* an attempt is made to give full and practical instruction in sabre and singlestick play, and in the use of sabre against bayonet, and also to explain the course of practice that is necessary for those who wish to perform the difficult sword feats which require at once strength and lightness of hand. How far I have succeeded in what I have sought to do it will be for the readers of these pages to judge; but I may perhaps be permitted to say that the book which I now venture to offer to the public is the result of experience in the use of arms extending over an unusually long period, and that before I began to teach, some twenty years ago, I was so fortunate as to be trained by teachers of the highest skill.

I learnt fencing from the late M. Prevost, Fencing-Master to H.R.H. the Prince of Wales, and to the Royal Family of France, and, as pupil and assistant, practised for many years with this admirable master of the small sword, who in his *prime* had been certainly one of the best fencers, perhaps the best, fencer in Paris. To make me as thorough a proficient with the weapon as he was himself, my esteemed friend spared no pains. In the use of the sabre and singlestick I was first trained by Mr. Platts, who had learnt from the celebrated Bushman his system of broadsword play.

I thus had the advantage of learning from those best qualified to teach; but when, after no short or easy period of probation, I became in my turn an instructor, and gained that knowledge which can only be gained by teaching and by constant combat with adversaries of all degrees of strength, it appeared to me that that part of the course I had gone through had been somewhat conventional, and though the system of fencing which I had learnt from Prevost could scarcely be altered for the better, the English method of sabre play, good as it was, could be considerably improved. Sabre-players, as a rule, have not been fencers, or at least have been fencers of trifling skill. Accomplished fencers have usually, from an exaggerated fear of losing their lightness of hand, not cared to work much with the sabre. The consequence has been that no attempt has been made to bring knowledge of the small sword to bear upon sabre play, and that little attention has been given to what is really the most formidable way of handling the latter weapon.

Those who have taught its use seem to have thought of little else than the cuts which can be given with it, and to have overlooked the fact that the modern sabre, essentially a cut-and-thrust weapon, can be used with great effect for thrusts, and that, when thrusting, a man exposes himself less and is more likely to disable his antagonist than when he delivers a cut. It is true that one or two thrusts have been taught, but small reliance has been placed in them, and several of the fencer's methods of attack and defence which are admirably suited for sword play have been altogether neglected.

Daily combats gave me every opportunity for putting my ideas to the rough test of practice, and I soon found that I was not mistaken, and that there were *longes* and time thrusts which could be delivered with the sword, and were formidable even to the most skilled opponents. I made it, therefore, part of my work as a teacher and sabre player to improve sabre play by adapting to it many movements used in fencing which have hitherto been entirely overlooked by sabre players, and also by copying the fencer to make the attacks, &c., in a closer and consequently quicker and more effective manner than they had before been made.

These movements are specially described in this *Manual*.

That the man who has mastered them will have a more varied and effective manner of using his weapon than one who has only practised the ordinary method, and will therefore be a far more formidable antagonist, will, I think, be admitted by all who, possessing some knowledge of the subject, do me the honour of giving attention to these pages; and inasmuch as sabre practice is not a mere exercise, but a course of training which teaches a man how to defend his life, it is scarcely necessary to point out that a really efficacious and not traditional method of using the weapon should be adopted.

Recent events have shown our soldiers that even in these days of "arms of precision" the sword is not by any means obsolete. Assuredly these men should be taught to handle it in the best way. A soldier's life may often depend on his being able to wield his sword against a determined antagonist, and his chances of victory are not likely to be improved by the fact that his instructors have forgotten that a sabre has a point as well as an edge, and have not taught him the most formidable way of using the weapon they have placed in his hands.

It is true that to many of those who learn how to handle the sabre this matter is not of much importance, inasmuch as what they seek is a healthy and interesting exercise, and as they are not likely to have to wield the weapon in the defence of their lives. Considered, however, merely as an amusement and an exercise, sabre play is better when the conditions of the actual combat are followed as closely as possible in the mimic fight.

It is more interesting and seems more real and practical, while the many varied movements which are required when every possible way of handling the sword is resorted to strengthen the whole frame as no other exercise can. I am not without hope that the altered system of sword play I have described in this *Manual* will, if properly followed, be found interesting by amateurs as well as by soldiers, and I am greatly encouraged in this hope by the fact that the very numerous pupils I have had the honour of instructing have never failed to take great interest in what they had to learn and practise: have often been as anxious to acquire complete mastery over the weapon as if they were shortly to use it in actual fight, and, in not a few cases, have attained exceptional proficiency. I would add that, while greatly changing the method of using the point in sabre play, I have been careful to retain all that was good in the old system, and have described minutely and to the best of my ability the established cuts and guards.

In these chapters I have written nothing special on Singlestick, as the stick is merely a substitute for the sabre, and is used exactly in the same manner, and throughout the *Manual* everything said about sword play applies equally to singlestick play.

On contests with sword against bayonet, nothing, so far as I am aware, has yet been written, and as the knowledge of how to use one weapon against another cannot but be of the greatest value to the soldier, I have endeavoured to put into the most practical form what I have learnt from observation of assaults innumerable, and from many hard struggles against vigorous antagonists.

Sword feats are of less importance than skill in the defensive and offensive use of the weapon, but when well performed are always greatly admired; and I have frequently found that good swordsmen were anxious to learn how to execute them. I have therefore carefully described the manner of accomplishing a variety of these *tours de force*. Some of these, such as—Cutting a sheep in two at one stroke, and, cutting an apple in a handkerchief without injuring the latter,

Are of my own invention, and I venture to say with confidence that any one possessed of a fair amount of strength, and accustomed to the use of the weapon, will be able, after some practice, to perform all the sword feats which are mentioned.

In conclusion, I trust I may be allowed, not in the usual formal manner, but as an assurance of respectful regard, to dedicate this little book to my pupils, whose attention and intelligence have yielded me unceasing encouragement, and to whose kind suggestion that I should put my system of instruction into a written form, these pages are due.

I have had the honour of instructing the following Clubs in both Fencing and Sabre:—

The London Fencing Club.

The Honourable Artillery Company, who, on my resignation after being with them upwards of twenty years, presented me with a very handsome testimonial.

The London Athletic Club.

The London Scottish V.R.C.

The 37th Middlesex V.R.C.

The 1st Middlesex Artillery.
&c., &c., &c.

The following gentlemen, all of whom were my pupils, have won the undermentioned prizes in open competition:—

1876.—London Athletic Club Cups for Fencing—1st. G. White, Esq. 2nd. R. Pullman, Esq.

1877.—London Athletic Club Cups for Fencing—1st. P. K. Rodger, Esq. 2nd. R. Pullman, Esq.

1877.—London Athletic Club Cups for Singlestick—1st. R. Hazard, Esq. 2nd. T. Wace, Esq.

1878.—London Athletic Club Cups for Singlestick—1st. H. H. Romilly, Esq. 2nd. R. Hazard, Esq.

1877.—German Gymnastic Society's Foils for Fencing—1st. H. Hartjen, Esq.

1878.—German Gymnastic Society's Foils for Fencing—1st.

H. Hartjen, Esq.

1878.—German Gymnastic Society's Prize for Singlestick—1st. R. Hazard, Esq.

1879.—German Gymnastic Society's Prize for Fencing—1st. H. Hartjen, Esq.

J. M. Waite.

19, Brewer Street,
Golden Square, London, W.
December, 1880.

Lessons in Sabre, Singlestick, &c.

How to Hold a Sabre.

In holding a light sabre, place the fingers round the grip so that the middle knuckles are in a line with the edge, and let the thumb lie on the back to enable you to direct the point.

With a heavy sabre, the thumb should be placed round the grip, or you may be disarmed by a strong beat made with a sword of the same weight.

In singlestick, do not let the end of the thumb touch the hilt, or a hard blow on the hilt might seriously injure it.

Hold the sword securely, but do not grasp it tightly, or your hand and arm will soon tire. The grasp should only be tightened when delivering a cut or forming a guard.

There is great art in easing the grip directly after a movement has been executed. A swordsman who does this properly has what is termed "a soft hand," a great desideratum in sword play. It gives quickness to the hand, and saves it from being jarred.

PLATE 1.—PRELIMINARY POSITION.

Sabre

Plate 1.

Turn the left foot to the left, and place the right in front of it, so that the back of the right heel touches the inside of the left. The feet will then be at right angles. Easing the grip, let the back of the sword rest in the hollow of the right shoulder, the sword-elbow touching the right hip, and the hand in a direct line in front of it. Close the left hand, and place it on the back of the left hip (so that it cannot be seen from the front), with the elbow thrown back.

Body half turned to the left, face full to the front.

PLATE 2.—ENGAGING GUARD.

PLATE 2

ENGAGING GUARD.

Move the sword-arm to the front until the hand is directly opposite the hollow of the right shoulder, bend the elbow slightly and raise it, sink the wrist, and turn up the middle knuckles and edge of the sword. Advance, and lower the point until it is nearly opposite and level with the left hip.

Then advance the right foot about twice its own length straight to the front, and at the same time bend both knees *well*. Keep the body and head upright, and divide their weight equally between both legs, with the loins well pressed in.

When this guard is properly formed, the upper knuckles and elbow are level and in line with the shoulder. It is called *High Seconde*.

On crossing swords, which should be about nine inches from each other's point, when it is called an equal engagement, press your blade gently upon that of your adversary, so as to close the line in which you are engaged. By this means you are protected from a straight thrust.

I prefer this Engaging Guard to any other for the following reasons:—

That when properly formed, it protects the arm and body from all cuts, and the sword is in the best position to defend the head and leg, which may be done by merely raising and lowering the hand. In other guards you have to turn the point down in addition to doing so.

Simply raising or lowering the hand will also parry the thrusts, however high or low or at whatever part they may be aimed. *Tierce* and *quarte*, which are the other engaging guards usually taken, only defend the right and left breasts.

The hand and point are also better placed in it than in other guards for giving the stop thrusts and time thrusts by opposition, and all attacks except those directed at the head.

The Engaging Guard with the point up is, however, preferred and taken by some sabre players. It is called outside guard or *tierce* when the hand is on the right, and inside guard or *quarte* when on the left side of the body. In each of these guards one side of the arm is exposed, and for that and the above-named reasons I do not like either of them so well as the one with the point down (*high seconde*).

To form the Inside Guard or *Quarte*.

Place the right elbow about eight inches in front of the centre of the right breast, with the hand advanced and to the left. Pommel of the sword opposite the left nipple. The point as high as, and about two or three inches to the right (his right) of your adversary's right eye. Edge slightly turned to your left.

To form the Outside Guard or *Tierce*.

Move the hand about six or seven inches to the right without shifting the upper arm, which should be kept near the side, and slightly turn the palm down. Edge to the right. Point about two or three inches to the left (his left) of your adversary's left eye. Hand and point the same height as in Inside Guard.

These guards may be used as parries with good effect against a bayonet or lance.

An Engaging Guard formed in the manner above described is called "Defensive," as it covers the side on which you are engaged, and defends it from a straight thrust.

It is called "Offensive" when the arm is more straightened and the point directed to your adversary, so that the line in which you are engaged is open.

After engaging, you are not bound to remain with the blades touching, but it is an advantage to do so to a man who possesses a light hand and has a fine feel of the blade.

The feel of the blade often telegraphs to you your adversary's intention. By it you can tell if he is going to attack, or you may learn what guard he will form on the first movement of your attack upon him.

To obtain a proper feel of the blade, you should not grasp your sword tightly, but gently press the tips of your fingers on the grip, and keep as light a touch of your adversary's blade as possible.

To Advance.

Move the right foot about six inches forward, letting the heel touch the ground first, then let the left foot follow it the same distance.

To Retire.

Move the left foot back about six inches, and let the right follow it the same distance.

In advancing or retiring, keep the head and body erect and perfectly steady, with the knees well bent.

To Attack.

Stretch the sword-arm to its full length as quickly as possible on a level with the shoulder, without stiffness or jerking or any preliminary movement, and direct the edge or point of your sword to the part you wish to hit. Raise the toes of the right foot, and step straight to the front, until the feet are about four times the length of your foot apart; let the heel touch the ground first.

As you raise the foot to *longe* press in the left haunch and straighten the left leg, keeping the left foot firmly fixed on the ground. In *longeing*, let the right heel almost touch the ground.

★★★★★★★★★★

Pressing in the left haunch when *longeing* adds considerable quickness to the attack, it also causes the body to be upright on the completion of the *longe*, and therefore enables a man to recover to the guard with less effort and greater quickness.

★★★★★★★★★★

On the completion of the *longe* the body and head should be erect, the shoulders have their natural fall, and the right knee be perpendicular to the instep, left leg straight, and foot flat and firm on the ground, and the weight of the body equally divided between the haunches. The whole of these movements should be performed *together* with the greatest rapidity.

Be careful not to give any sign of preparation, but make the attack with great boldness and suddenness.

Do not raise the hand, or draw it or the point of the sword back when about to deliver an attack; by so doing you expose your arm to a time cut and the body to a time thrust.

In attacking, never let the foot touch the ground before the sword reaches its destination.

In all attacks and returns the point of the sword should travel over no more space than is necessary for it to arrive at its intended destination.

To Recover.

Draw back the arm and foot, and bending the left knee, resume the position of Guard, with knees well bent.

Opposition.

Is to oppose your sword to that of your adversary when cutting or thrusting, either in an attack or return, so as to prevent him from touching you, at the same time in the same line, with a counter.

Thus, if you deliver a cut on the left side of his head, bear your hand to your own left until it is as high as, and about four inches to the left of, your eye; the left side of your head will then be guarded.

In like manner, always cover with the *forte* of your sword the part of your own person which corresponds with the part you are attacking.

While cutting at your adversary's left side or thrusting with your palm turned up in *quarte*, your hand should be opposite your left shoulder. While cutting at his right side or thrusting with the palm turned down in *tierce*, your hand should be opposite your right shoulder.

The elevation of the hand depends on where the attack is made, but it ought rarely to be below the shoulder, except when cutting at the leg.

Against a man who counters on the head, the hand should be kept as high as your own eye.

If you neglect your opposition, you are liable to be both guarded and hit at the same time by a man who counters with good opposition.

PLATE 3

FEINTING.

A feint is a threatened attack made to induce your adversary to guard one part while you deliver the real attack on another. It is made by suddenly straightening the arm, without any movement of the body or feet, and directing the point at the place you wish him to guard.

Feints are also made to find out a man's method of defence and general style of play; when done for that purpose you should watch carefully what he does, and instantly return to your guard, but when it is your intention to follow up the feint with an attack the cut should follow the feint with the greatest rapidity.

An attack preceded by a feint is done thus: Make the feint as directed above, then *longe*, and by a quick and close action of the wrist, deliver the real attack, taking care not to draw back the hand as you do so.

This is called "Deceiving a Guard."

GUARDS.

All guards should be made with the edge of the *forte* of the sword, that is, the half of the blade next to the hand (the other half is called the feeble), and with the wrist well sunk. A firm guard is thus formed, and consequently a quick return can be given.

Too much force should not be used, so that a second guard may be readily made should the first be deceived. The sword should never be moved one inch more than is necessary to defend the part attacked.

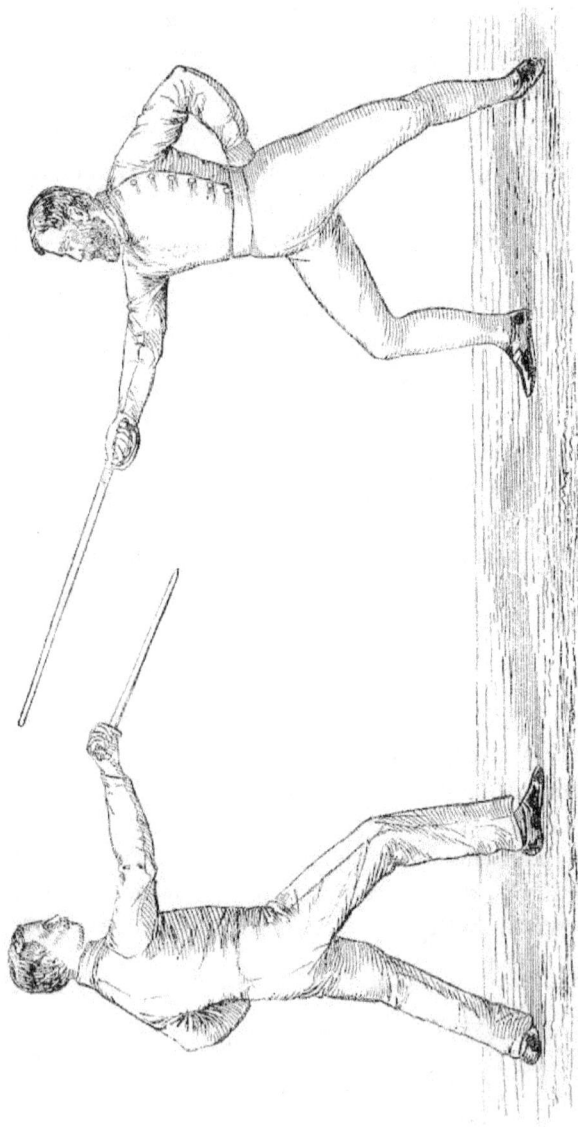

PLATE 3.—FEINT AT THE HEAD.

PLATE 4

A DIRECT LEAD OFF AT THE HEAD AND GUARD.

This is the only direct cut in leading off that can be made with any degree of safety on a man who forms the engaging guard, shown in Plate 2.

It can be given in five different directions, *viz.*:—

Horizontally on the right side of the head.
Ditto on the left side of the head.
Diagonally on the right temple.
Ditto on the left temple.

I prefer the cuts on the left side of the head, for the reasons that the extra turn of the wrist necessary for their execution adds considerable force to them, and that when the opposition is correctly formed the whole of the head is defended from a counter, which is not the case when the cuts are delivered on the right side. Then the opposition only covers that side of the head. This I think to be of great importance, as the head, as a rule, is the part at which men naturally and generally counter. The vertical is not an effective one. A downward cut on the top of a man's head protected by a helmet would not do him much harm.

In making the horizontal or diagonal cut at the right side of the head, a man may be timed if his adversary, instead of guarding, gives a straight thrust with his hand opposite his right eye as the attack is being made. The opposition thus formed would guard the attack. This cannot be done on the cuts at the left side of the head, as there is no certain opposition on that side.

The diagonal cut at the left side of the head should be aimed at the temple in such a direction that, should the sword pass through, it would come out near the right angle of the jaw. (In actual combat I should aim the diagonal and horizontal cuts between the ear and the top of the jacket collar.)

It should be made with the wrist, and delivered in the manner described earlier in To Attack.

PLATE 4.—A DIRECT LEAD OFF AT THE HEAD AND GUARD (PRIME).

Be careful as you *longe* to bear your hand to the left, so that, as you strike the head, your hand is as high as, and a little to the left of, your left eye and look over your forearm.

Guard for the Head (*Prime*).

Raise the hand until it is opposite the right temple, with the upper knuckles level with the top of the head, so that you can see under the *forte* of the sword without lowering the chin. Point well advanced, and nearly opposite to the left elbow, so as to cover the left cheek and breast. Edge upwards. Arm slightly bent, with elbow turned up and hidden behind the hilt.

A short man should form this guard a little higher than the right temple.

Feint a Straight Thrust at the Breast, and Cut at the Head.

Feint a straight thrust at your adversary's breast under his blade, by suddenly straightening the arm, with the hand as high as the shoulder, and hilt turned upwards to protect the arm from a time cut; then, without lowering the hand or drawing back the point, *longe* and deliver the diagonal cut on the left temple.

This attack is sometimes made by feinting at the outside of the leg instead of at the breast. It is not, however, so safe, as you expose the arm to a time cut while making it.

PLATE 5

FEINT AT THE HEAD AND CUT AT THE LEFT CHEEK AND GUARD.

This can only be done when a man forms his head guard with the point too high. Feint a cut at the head by straightening the arm and directing the point to a little above the centre of the forehead, edge of the sword turned downwards. Then, with the action of the wrist, and without touching your adversary's blade, pass the sword to your right until you have cleared his point, and with a *longe* deliver a cut on his left cheek just below the ear, the edge of the sword slightly turned up so that the arm may be covered with the hilt.

Opposition the same as in the diagonal cut at the head (as in Plate 4).

This cut may be given without being preceded by a feint, when the adversary forms his head guard with the point drawn back and high.

GUARD FOR THE FEINT AT THE HEAD AND CUT AT THE LEFT CHEEK.

The guard for the head, described in Plate 4, will stop this attack, but should you find your opponent is passing his sword under your point, lower your hand quickly and bear it to your left until the pommel is opposite your left nipple. Point as high as the top of your head and a little to the left of your hand, edge to the left, wrist sunk, and inside of forearm resting on the body, to prevent the cut being given under the wrist.

This is the *quarte* guard with the hand drawn a little back. It may also be used against returns at the left breast.

PLATE 5.—FEINT AT THE HEAD AND CUT AT THE LEFT CHEEK, AND GUARD (*QUARTE*).

PLATE 6

FEINT AT THE HEAD AND CUT AT THE LEFT BREAST, AND GUARD.

This is done under the same circumstances and in the same manner as "The Feint at the Head and Cut at the Left Cheek," except that the cut is aimed at the left nipple. Opposition the same as when cutting at the head.

The guard, also, is the same, except that the hand should be a little lower when forming the *quarte*.

In the illustration the guard is formed with the point down (*prime*).

Plate 6.—Feint at the Head and Cut at the Left Breast, and Guard (*Prime*).

Plate 7

Feint at the Head and Cut Inside the Wrist.

This is also done under the same circumstances and in the same manner as "The Feint at the Head and Cut at the Left Cheek," except that you only make a half *longe*, and aiming at the inside of the wrist, make a retrograde cut by drawing your hand towards your body, and at the same time retire out of distance to avoid the counter.

The guard for this attack is the same as the one for "The Feint at the Head and Cut at the Left Cheek."

None of the three preceding attacks can be made on a man who keeps the point of his sword well down and forward when guarding the head or left breast, and who does not attempt to return until he has found his opponent's blade.

The head guard, as described in Plate 4, will guard the left cheek and wrist, and the engaging guard with the edge a little turned to your left will defend the cut at the left breast. They should, as a rule, be used against all attacks directed against these parts.

The guard with the point up ought only to be used as an auxiliary, when you find that your point in forming the other guard has got too high.

If you always use it to defend the left side, you may easily be hit by a feint at the left and a cut at the right side or forearm.

PLATE 7.—FEINT AT THE HEAD AND CUT AT THE INSIDE OF THE WRIST.

PLATE 8

FEINT AT THE HEAD AND CUT UNDER THE RIGHT ARM, AND GUARD.

This attack, when well executed, is most difficult to judge and guard.

Feint at the head by suddenly straightening the arm and directing the point to a little above your adversary's forehead, with the edge of the sword turned down, then, without drawing back the arm, but with the action of the wrist only, *longe* and deliver a cut on the right armpit, the edge slightly turned up so that the arm may be covered with the hilt. Always aim this cut high, so that should your adversary form his guard a little low you will hit the outside of his shoulder.

Opposition, hand as high as and opposite to your right shoulder.

The cut may sometimes be given on the arm.

GUARD FOR THE CUT UNDER THE RIGHT ARM.

Should you have been induced to answer the feint and form the head guard, lower the hand again as quickly as possible to the engaging guard, with the edge of the sword turned a little to your right.

PLATE 8.—FEINT AT THE HEAD AND CUT UNDER RIGHT ARM, AND GUARD (HIGH *SECONDE*).

PLATE 9

FEINT AT THE HEAD AND CUT OUTSIDE THE LEG, AND GUARD.

This is done under the same circumstances and in the same manner as "The Feint at the Head and Cut under the Right Arm," except that you aim the cut at the leg a little below the knee, or you may make the feint by threatening a thrust at the breast over the blade.

Opposition to your right, and as high as possible.

GUARD FOR OUTSIDE LEG (*SECONDE*).

Drop the hand as low as the right hip and a little to the right of it. Point advanced as in the other guards and about 16 inches from the ground. Edge upwards.

Plate 9.—Feint at the Head and Cut Outside the Leg, and Guard (*Seconde*).

PLATE 10

A FEINT AT THE BREAST AND CUT INSIDE THE LEG.

Feint a thrust at your adversary's breast over his blade, and as he raises his guard, pass your point to your right, and without touching his blade, clear his point and deliver a cut inside his leg above the knee with a *longe*.

Opposition to your left and as high as possible.

ANOTHER WAY OF ATTACKING INSIDE OF LEG.

Beat your adversary's sword to your right, then suddenly straighten your arm, and turning the edge inwards, *longe* and deliver a cut on the inside of his leg.

Opposition to your left, and as high as possible.

GUARD FOR INSIDE OF LEG.

The same as for outside of leg, except that you move your hand to the left until it hangs over the right knee.

PLATE 10.—FEINT AT THE BREAST AND CUT INSIDE THE LEG, AND GUARD.

PLATE 11

SHIFTING THE LEG TO AVOID A CUT, AND COUNTERING ON THE HEAD.

As your adversary cuts at your leg, draw it quickly back and assume the first position shown in Plate 1, and at the same time deliver a diagonal cut on his head or arm, with good opposition, so that should your adversary feint at your leg and cut at the head, the opposition will guard his attack. Be careful not to raise the hand in making the counter. This manoeuvre may also be used against attacks made at the left breast.

PLATE 11.—Shifting the Leg to Avoid a Cut and Counter on the Head.

PLATE 12

SHIFTING THE LEG WHEN A MAN ATTACKS WITH HIS HAND
BELOW THE SHOULDER, AND COUNTER ON THE ARM.

The above manoeuvre may be executed on any cut or thrust given with the hand below the shoulder, except that the counter should be aimed at the inside of the arm and the left foot moved back about eight inches before drawing up to the first position, so that you are out of distance.

The counter will act as a half circular parry should you not reach the arm.

The counter on the head or arm can also be given when a man returns at the leg after guarding his head. In this case you must recover in one movement from the *longe* to the first position, and at the same time deliver the counter.

It is much more difficult to recover from the *longe* than from the guard with sufficient quickness to avoid a return, but practice and good position on the *longe* will enable any one with good legs to accomplish it.

PLATE 12.—Shifting the Leg When a Man Attacks With His Hand Below the Shoulder, and Counter on the Arm.

PLATE 13

A DRAW AND GUARD FOR SHIFTING THE LEG TO AVOID A CUT
AND COUNTER ON THE HEAD OR ARM.

Feint a cut at outside leg, then *longe*, and forming the head guard,
receive his counter on your sword and deliver a return under his right
arm.

Plate 13.—A Draw and Guard for Shifting the Leg and Counter on the Head or Arm.

Plate 14

A Draw and Stop for Shifting the Leg to avoid a Cut and Counter on the Head or Arm.

Feint at outside of leg, and as your adversary tries to counter, make a half *longe*, and, aiming at the inside of his wrist, make a retrograde cut by drawing your hand towards your body, and at the same time retire out of distance.

Attacks at the leg should never be made without being preceded by a feint or a beat to divert your adversary's attention, and even when done in that manner you should be chary of their use. The man on the defensive has the advantage of either guarding and returning or shifting and countering, and should he adopt the latter method and not shift his leg quickly enough to avoid the hit, he would have considerably the better of the exchange.

I do not, however, think that attacks at the leg should be entirely ignored, neither do I think that they should always be avoided by shifting the leg. A man on horseback cannot do so. Both methods of defence should be practised. A man who relies entirely upon shifting may easily be drawn into a trap, as is shown in Plates 13 and 14. When mounted, the leg guards defend your horse as well as your leg.

Returns at the leg may be made without much fear of being countered.

PLATE 14.—A DRAW AND STOP FOR SHIFTING THE LEG AND COUNTER ON THE HEAD OR ARM.

Feint and Cut at the Arm.

Feint at the right temple and deliver a cut under the forearm, or feint at the outside of the leg and cut at the top of the forearm.

Guard for the Arm.

The Engaging Guard.

Should your adversary form his engaging guard with his hand higher than his shoulder, pass the point of your sword suddenly between his *forte* and wrist, and, turning the edge, deliver a drawing cut on the inside of his wrist, retiring out of distance as you do so.

Plate 15

Guard for an Upward Cut at the Fork.

This is not a good cut, and I do not recommend its use. To guard it, draw the right leg up to the first position, and at the same time form the outside leg guard.

Straight Thrust.

When on guard, the point of your sword is under the *forte* of your adversary's, and a straight thrust may be given should he quit the engagement, by suddenly straightening the arm and directing the point at his breast; deliver it with a *longe*.

A good time to make this thrust is when he prepares for his attack or dwells on his feint at your head, or when he advances, as described later on.

The guard for the straight thrust is the same as that used for guarding the outside of the leg.

Thrust by Disengaging over the Blade.

This is given in the same manner and under the same circumstances as the straight thrust, except that you pass the point of your sword over the *forte* of your adversary's.

These thrusts may be given either with the palm of the hand turned down in *tierce*, when the hand should be opposite to your right shoulder, or with the palm turned up in *quarte*, when the hand should be opposite your left shoulder.

In both thrusts the edge of the sword should be well turned up, so that the hand and arm are covered by the hilt, and the point brought in line with the adversary's breast.

As the point touches, the hand should rise and the grip of the sword be slightly eased, the arm kept perfectly straight and well stretched.

It is dangerous to thrust when practising with sabres, unless you are well protected with pads; but with sticks the point should be freely used, always, however, taking care to ease the grip as the point touches, so that your hand may slip a little up the stick, and by that means avoid

PLATE 15.—GUARD FOR AN UPWARD CUT AT THE FORK.

giving your adversary an unpleasant prod.

The guard for the thrust over the blade is the same as that used for guarding the head.

Feint a Straight Thrust and Disengage over the Blade.

Straighten your arm and threaten a straight thrust, and without bending the arm or drawing it back, disengage over the blade and deliver the thrust with a *longe*.

To Guard this Attack.

Form the outside leg guard, and then the head guard, as quickly, lightly, and closely as possible.

"One, Two."

Pass your point over your adversary's blade, and with a straight arm threaten a thrust, then, instantly, without bending the arm or drawing it back, pass your point under his sword and deliver a thrust with a *longe*.

To guard this attack, form the head guard and then the outside leg guard.

Attacks made with an Advance.

All the attacks can be preceded by an advance. When so done, the movement should be covered with a beat either under or over the adversary's blade, to prevent a stop thrust being given. The beat should be made very closely with the thumb and forefinger, and both it and the feint should be done while advancing, and the cut or thrust given with the *longe*.

★★★★★★★★★★

The beat may also be used with great advantage in attacks not preceded by an advance. It should be made when a counter is expected, which it would most probably prevent, and should occasionally be used to check the adversary's parry.

★★★★★★★★★★

In the advance and *longe* the right foot moves twice and the left once. They should move as quickly as it is possible to count "One, two, three."

A short man ought to use this method of attack when opposed to a tall man, as otherwise he cannot reach him. He should advance very rapidly, with short steps, and be prepared to parry as he goes forward should his beat be deceived.

A tall man ought seldom or never to advance when attacking.

RETURNS.

Returns should be made with a *longe* with the greatest rapidity after guarding. Great care must be taken not to draw back the hand or point before making them.

They should, as a rule, be made direct, but may sometimes be preceded by a feint, and should be very much varied.

The best returns from the different guards are the following, placed in the order of their comparative merits, that is, the first is a better return than the second, and so on; but their application should depend a great deal on your adversary's defence:—

FROM GUARDING THE HEAD.

Cut at the head.
Do. Under the right arm.
Thrust at breast with palm down (*tierce*).
Cut at outside the leg.
Do. Left breast.
Do. Inside the leg.

FROM GUARDING THE RIGHT SIDE UNDER THE ARM.

Cut at the head.
Thrust at breast with palm down (*tierce*).
Cut under the right arm.
Do. on outside the leg.
Do. on left breast.
Do. on inside the leg

FROM GUARDING THE LEFT BREAST WITH THE POINT OF THE SWORD DOWN (*PRIME*).

Cut at the head.
Thrust at the breast with palm turned up (*quarte*).
Cut under the right arm.
Do. on outside the leg.
Do. on left breast.
Do. on inside the leg

From Guarding the Left Breast or Left Cheek with the Point up (*Quarte*).

Thrust at the breast with palm turned up (*quarte*).
Cut at right cheek or neck (horizontal)
Do. at head (left diagonal).
Do. under right arm.
Do. outside of leg.
Do. left breast.
Do. inside the leg.

From Guarding Outside of the Leg.

Cut at the right side of the head, neck or shoulder.
Thrust at the breast (palm turned down).
Cut at the inside of leg
Do. under right arm.
Do. left breast.
Do. outside of leg.
Do. left horizontal at head. As you form the guard draw back your sword until it is clear of your adversary's point, and deliver a horizontal cut on the left side of his head.

From Guarding the Inside of Leg.

Thrust at the breast (palm turned up).
Cut at the head
Do. under right arm.
Do. outside of leg.
Do. left breast.
Do. inside the leg

From Guarding the Thrust under the Blade.

Make the returns as from guarding outside of the leg.

From Guarding the Thrust over the Blade.

Make the returns as from guarding the head.

Returns at the arm should always be made when an opportunity is given.

Stop Thrusts.

A stop thrust is given, when a man advances with his attack. Immediately you see him move, deliver a straight thrust at his breast with a *longe*; you will then, if your movement is done in proper time, find your point on his breast as he has completed the advance, and he will be unable to *longe* and deliver his attack.

To prevent this thrust being made on you, beat under your adversary's blade as you advance.

PLATE 16

To Deceive the Beat under the Blade (*QUARTE* Thrust).

As your adversary advances with a beat, pass your point over the *forte* of his blade, and thus avoiding his beat, *longe* and deliver the thrust.

To Avoid This.

Instead of beating under the blade as you advance, pass your point over the blade and beat down.

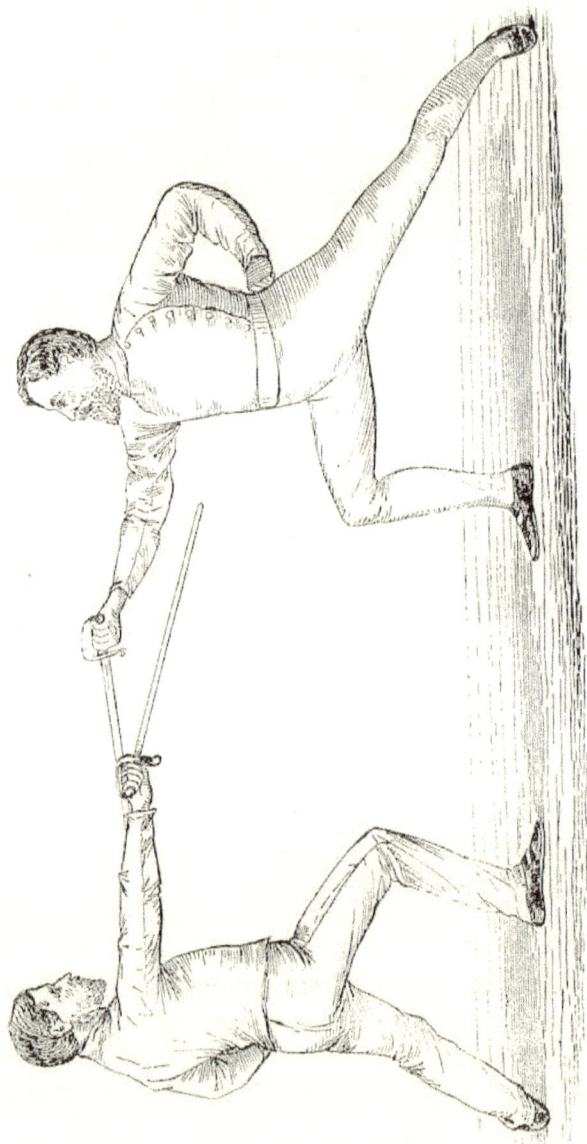

Plate 16.—To Deceive the Beat Under the Blade (Quarte Thrust).

PLATE 17

STOP CUT AFTER DECEIVING THE BEAT OVER THE BLADE.

As he advances with a beat over your blade, draw your arm back, and, avoiding his sword, deliver a cut at his head, or a thrust at his breast, with a *longe*.

★★★★★★★★★★

If it should unfortunately occur that you have to defend yourself with an ordinary stick against a man similarly armed, he will probably seek to disarm you by cutting at your hand. Deceive him by offering the hand, and on his cut, draw it back, and cut straight at his head. His blow will fall harmlessly, and the effect of yours will be considerably confusing to him.

★★★★★★★★★★

This may also be done on a man who attacks your sword, or who makes short cuts at your head. On such occasions you must be careful to draw your hand towards your right temple, so that should he make a real attack your head would be guarded.

Stop thrusts may also be used with great effect on a man who retires as you lead off at him, and then advances before making his return.

To do them under these circumstances, you must be very quick on your legs, so as to be able to recover to your guard and deliver the thrust as he advances.

If you are not quick enough to do this, make a false attack with a half *longe* and draw him; you will then have more time.

TO DRAW THE STOP THRUST AND STOP CUT.

These may be drawn and parried thus: Advance as if you intended to attack, but instead of doing so parry the thrust and return quickly.

PLATE 17.—STOP CUT AFTER DECEIVING THE BEAT OVER THE BLADE.

Plate 18

Immediately you see him move, *longe* and deliver a straight thrust, or you may give the thrust without longing, by merely straightening the arm. I prefer, however, to *longe* with the thrust, as it is more certain to stop the attack.

Stop thrusts, to be successful, should be given without hesitation and with the greatest boldness.

PLATE 18.—Stop Thrust (*Tierce*) When a Man Draws His Hand Back to Attack.

Remise.

A *remise* is a sort of time hit made on the *longe*, when a man after guarding delays his return. It is done thus: Immediately after you have delivered your attack, draw your hand and head back to simulate a recovery, and without moving the foot, make a second hit at the same place as rapidly as possible.

Unless this hit is given decidedly before the return is made, the hit counts to the one who returns.

Renewal of the Attack or Redoubling.

A redouble is a renewal of the attack when your adversary after guarding does not return. It should be done with great rapidity and in a different line to that of the first attack.

Reprise Attack.

A *reprise* is a sudden repetition of the attack, after a phrase in which no hit has been got and both have returned to the guard. It must be done with great quickness, so as to catch your adversary a little un-prepared.

PLATE 19.—TIME THRUST WITH OPPOSITION.

PLATE 19

TIME THRUST WITH OPPOSITION.

A time thrust can be made when a man feints at your head and tries to deliver a cut under your right arm, or on any part of the right side down to the foot.

As he raises his point to feint, make a straight thrust at his breast with a *longe*, keeping your hand as high as your right shoulder and a little to the right of it. Palm turned down.

Should you be quick enough, your point will fix on his breast, and his cut will fall on the *forte* of your sword.

If you are too slow, your thrust will guard his attack, although you may not touch him.

The same movements should be executed on the adversary, when from the engagement of *High Seconde* he endeavours to deceive *prime*, or, when from that of *tierce*, he tries to deceive *quarte* with "One, Two."

ANOTHER TIME THRUST.

When from the engagement of *quarte* he attempts to deceive *tierce* by a "One, Two," lower your point on his first movement, and bearing your hand to your right, deliver a thrust on his right flank with a *longe*. Hand to your right and palm turned down.

TO DRAW AND STOP A TIME THRUST.

Feint a cut at the head or a thrust over the blade, and instead of delivering a cut or thrust, parry the thrust, and return with a half *longe*.

PLATE 20

A Time Cut.

When a man raises his hand or draws it back to lead off, hit him on the outside of the wrist and get away out of distance.

In using the stop thrusts, *remises*, and time thrusts, great judgment is required. They should never be attempted until the swordsman has had considerable experience. When given at the proper time, they are beautiful and effective strokes, but when badly timed, great danger attends their use, and mutual hitting is often the result.

Young players will do well not to attempt them.

In an assault, should you find yourself timed and not know how to draw and stop a time thrust, your safest plan will be to make direct attacks only, that is, attacks not preceded by a feint.

PLATE 20.—Time Cut when a Man Raises His Hand to Attack.

DRAWING.

Is to induce your adversary to deliver a certain cut or thrust for which you are prepared. To do this, make a false attack, that is, attack with a half *longe* so that you can the more readily recover and guard; thus, having drawn out and guarded his cut, instantly deliver a genuine one.

To prevent this being done upon you, draw back your hand as your adversary makes his false attack, and thus avoiding his sword, deliver a cut on his head with a *longe* (*vide* Plate 17.).

OBSERVATIONS ON FEINTING.

When a man makes a feint on you and you foresee his intention, do not answer it, but wait and parry his last movement. When acting on this principle, take care he does not make a direct attack, for should he do so, you will be too late, as his arm would be straight before you have moved.

If you answer a feint, form your first guard as lightly and as correctly as possible, so that you have time to make a second one.

By not forming the first correctly, your adversary, taking advantage of your fault, would be able to hit you when otherwise he could not. The hits shown in Plates 5, 6, and 7 are got through this cause.

When you are in doubt about his intentions, step back out of distance on his first movement.

When a man will not answer your feints, make them with greater energy and rapidity, and thus force him to do so.

How to Deal with a Man who is Continually Countering.

When you meet with a man who is guilty of this very bad practice, you should deal with him in the following ways:—

Either act on the defensive and let him lead off, then after guarding, return as quickly as possible and get away.

Or, make false attacks, and thus draw out his counters, which guard, and then returning with great quickness, get away.

Or, by opposition, when, should his counters be directed at your head or left side, lead off without feinting with good opposition (in fact your opposition should be slightly exaggerated) at the part of his person which will correspond with that of your own at which you think he will aim his counter.

If his counters are directed at your right side, attack him with a straight thrust with your hand as high as, and a little to the right of, your right shoulder. Palm turned down.

WHEN OPPOSED TO A MAN WHO ENGAGES IN *QUARTE* OR *TIERCE*.

When opposed to a man who engages in *quarte* or *tierce*, you will find that he will guard his right cheek and side with *tierce*, and his left side with *quarte*. You may then make the following attacks in addition to those already shown:—

From the Engagement of Tierce.
Cut at the inside of his wrist.
Feint inside the wrist and cut at the outside.
Feint at the left cheek and cut at the right.
Feint at the left breast and cut at the right side or at his forearm.

From the Engagement of Quarte.
Cut at the outside of his wrist.
Feint outside the wrist and cut at the inside.
Feint at the right cheek and cut at the left.
Feint at the right side and cut at the left.

His stop thrust should be avoided in the following manner:—

To prevent him from giving you a straight thrust as you advance to attack, beat his blade either in *tierce* or *quarte*.

Should he avoid the beat by disengaging and thrust upon you, make a beat before you move the feet, then, as you advance, change quickly and beat on the other side of his blade, and instantly deliver your attack.

The beat will probably draw his disengagement, and the change will parry it.

To change is to pass your sword under that of your adversary, and rejoin the blades on the opposite line.

Observations.

On Countering and Hard-Hitting.

When you are making an assault with sabres or sticks, remember they are substitutes for sharp swords, and act as though every hit you would receive would either kill or disable you. All your movements must be governed by this idea. You should never attempt to do anything with a stick that you could or would not do with a sword.

You must remember that in an actual combat the sabres have sharp points and edges, and that a very light touch would probably place you *hors de combat*.

Hitting at your adversary when he is attacking you is almost as bad as cutting your own throat, for you are almost certain to be more or less seriously wounded; your chances of escape are very small indeed. You must, therefore, always endeavour to guard the attack and never counter except when you can avoid the hit by shifting.

You must never hit after you are hit, as it is very doubtful if you would be able to do so with sharp swords.

The act of countering, so deservedly popular among boxers, is not admissible here. A blow with the fist will probably only shake you, but with a sharp sword the effect would be much more serious. There is no such thing as give and take with that weapon, and I question if there is much in a serious encounter with sticks, as a well delivered blow on any part of the head would in all probability cause a cessation of hostilities.

Rough and heavy hitting should be avoided: it destroys quickness; greater effect is given to a hit by pace than by force.

A hard hitter has to brace himself together before attacking; he thus prepares, and while doing so may easily be hit.

If his attack is guarded, he cannot recover and guard a return so readily as he ought to do.

His returns are not given so quickly as they should be, for after guarding, he is almost certain to draw his hand back in order to make them with greater force.

As he hits, so he will guard; heaviness will pervade all his movements; therefore, if you deceive his guard, he cannot make a second one with sufficient quickness to stop a good attack, as he will throw too much force into the first.

Slowness is the natural result of heaviness, quickness that of lightness; therefore, if you wish to become a *bon tireur*, cultivate and practise light play.

In trying to play light, you must not get into the habit of making snatching hits by which you would only scratch your adversary. However lightly you deliver them, let them be so given that with a sharp sword they would be effective, and your points fixed so that they would penetrate.

Cut versus Thrust.

Some writers on the sword, acting on the presumption that the sword must be elevated in order to gain force before cutting, have asserted that the point traverses two-thirds less distance when thrusting than when cutting. If this were correct, the less use made of the cut the better, as a good swordsman would most certainly give a time cut on the arm or deliver a thrust on a man while he was thus preparing to cut.

I once saw a sketch drawn to prove this assertion, in which the man thrusting was depicted with his point lowered to a line with his adversary's breast instead of being level with his eye, while the man who was cutting, and should have had his sword similarly placed, had his point drawn back and raised about two feet above his head, a distance greater than I should draw the point of my sword back were I going to cut the carcase of a sheep in two at one stroke.

The point should not be drawn back or elevated when cutting either in an attack or in a return.

There is only one direct cut in leading off (that at the head), and that can be given with quite sufficient force without the slightest elevation of the point if the sword arm and leg act together.

In all other attacks and returns the feint, or the act of forming the guard, gives great impetus to the cut.

It has also been asserted that in making a thrust the sword moves in a straight line, and in making a cut it moves in a circle.

This assertion is erroneous, and having been made without contradiction, has been generally accepted as a fact, and hence become a popular error.

All straight thrusts and disengagements move in straight lines, but in the cut over, the point has to be drawn back before the thrust can be given, and when a cut over is made after a parry, the point traverses as great if not a greater distance than in any cut.

Compare the following movements, which I think are the longest made either in thrusting or cutting.

Engage with foils in *quarte* and parry the disengagement into *tierce*

68

with *prime*, and *riposte* with a cut over.

Engage with sabres in high *seconde*, and, guarding an attack at the head with *prime*, return at the inside of the leg.

All direct cuts at the right side on any part from head to foot, from whatever guards they are made, move in as straight lines as any thrusts that can be given, and are consequently as quick.

In all other cuts the point moves in a circle.

However partial one may be to the thrust, and I acknowledge that I am one of its partisans, justice should be given to the cut, and although it may not in every instance be so quick or so fatal in its effect as the thrust, it has its advantages. Among others, it rarely passes, that is, goes by the object aimed at, without touching it, as the thrust will often do, more particularly when aimed at the arm or leg.

Useful Hints.

Immediately you go on guard, touch your adversary's sword with yours, and retire out of distance to avoid a surprise. This is called "engaging."

Keep your eyes open and fixed upon your adversary, watching all his movements.

Hold yourself in as easy a manner as possible, particularly the sword arm.

Keep your knees well bent while setting to; you cannot *longe* quickly unless you do.

Move the feet lightly, and never drag them on the ground.

Be careful to always keep sufficient room behind you to be able to retire. Should your adversary try to drive you back, either attack him or threaten an attack.

While manoeuvring, keep out of reach, and plan your attacks and deliver them immediately you are within distance, then recover to the position of guard whether you have succeeded or not.

Should your adversary guard your attack and return, form the necessary guard, and make a second attack without the slightest delay.

Do not hit at the same place more than twice in succession, but vary your attacks and returns very much.

After two or three exchanges, break away out of distance to steady yourself and plan your next movements. In making long phrases you get slow and out of form, and, consequently, are not likely to get a hit.

Always deliver your cuts with a true edge and with the centre of percussion, which is generally about seven or eight inches from the point. It is the most effective part of the sword to cut with, and will not jar the arm like a cut made with any other part of the blade.

Never press upon your adversary's blade after having delivered a cut or thrust, but recover as quickly as possible to guard the return. Should he press upon yours, disengage and return as quickly as possible.

Make all your cuts with the wrist; never throw your arm out of line, but always keep it in front of you.

The action of cutting at your opponent's left side (called the inside line), is something like that of throwing, and at his right side (outside line) like that of whipping.

Always keep in front of your opponent, never more to your right or left; should he do so, keep on your own ground, turning only so much as to enable you to have your right toes pointed to his. Let him move round as much as he likes: he will only tire himself and gain no advantage.

Keep the head and body erect and quiet in all positions.

★★★★★★★★★★

The advantages of this are fully and clearly shown by that justly celebrated fencer, Captain G. Chapman, in his *Sequel to Foil Practice*.

★★★★★★★★★★

If you lean forward on the attack, a man much shorter than yourself can thrust you through the head by simply retiring and straightening his arm, while your attack would not reach him. You also cannot recover quickly, as too much weight is thrown upon the front leg.

Avoid remaining on the *longe* and getting to close quarters, no true defence can be made when in-fighting.

If you remain on the *longe*, your adversary may easily and without any danger step forward with his left foot and seize the wrist of your sword arm with his left hand. (Although this would not be permitted in a duel, a man would not hesitate to do it in actual combat). By always recovering to your guard such a manoeuvre is avoided, and, if attempted, you may easily deliver a straight thrust as he steps forward.

Another reason why you should always recover to your guard after an attack is, if you remain on the *longe* and your adversary retires one step, you cannot reach him; he has then the advantage of position, and will be able to attack you, while you can only act on the defensive.

If you can hit your adversary without feinting, do so, as it is more dangerous to make two motions than one.

Use judgment, study your opponent's play, and make no meaningless movements. An assault ought not to last longer than ten minutes. After that time, if you have fenced with energy and vigour, you lose your quickness and get out of form, and thereby contract slow and bad habits.

Exercises.

The following exercises may be practised by two advanced players. The hits and guards must be made as correctly, smartly, and as rapidly in succession as possible, taking it in turns to lead off. Care being taken not to move the left feet, and to strictly preserve the proper distance between you.

The following is an example of the way in which they should be gone through:—

We are both on guard, and in hitting distance.

I say, "You lead off."

Head, head, under right arm.

You then lead off at my head, which I guard and return with a *longe* at yours.

You recover, and guard your head, and then with a *longe* hit under my right arm, I guard.

We should then remain steady a few moments, you on the *longe* hitting under my right arm, I on guard defending my right side, to see if the positions of the sword arms, feet, and bodies are correct.

This should invariably be done at the finish of each exercise. It helps to keep you in form.

Another Example.

You say to me, "You lead off."

Feint head, and hit under right arm. Thrust at breast. Head.

I feint at your head, and cut under your right arm, which you guard, and *longeing*, return with a thrust at my breast.

I recover and parry it, then, with a *longe*, cut at your head. Both remain steady to see the positions.

1st Exercise.—Head. Head. Head.

2nd do.—Head. Head. Under right arm.

3rd do.—Head. Head. Outside leg.

4th do.—Head. Head. Left breast.

5th do.—Head. Head. Inside leg.

6th do.—Feint head, hit under right arm. Thrust at breast. Head.

7th do.—Feint head, hit outside leg. Thrust at breast. Head.

8th do.—Thrust straight at breast. Head. Hit under right arm.

9th do.—Disengage with a thrust. Hit under right arm. Head.

10th do.—Head. Head. Hit under right arm. Thrust at breast. Head.

11th do.—Head. Head. Hit outside leg. Thrust at breast. Head.

12th do.—Feint a thrust under the blade, and hit at the head. Inside leg. Thrust at the breast. Head. Head.

In these exercises you must not get into the habit of cutting only at each other's swords, and thereby making a mock combat, but you should try to hit each other on every occasion.

The Salute.

The Salute is a ceremony usually performed by two sabre players previous to making an assault. It is a mark of respect to those looking on, and an act of courtesy to each other.

Both should move together, and keep correct time throughout its performance.

There is no established method, but the following is that generally adopted by the best sabre players I know.

The two adversaries, facing each other in the first position, without wearing masks, which should be laid on the floor on their left, go smartly on guard, as shown in Plate 2, and having beat twice on each other's blades, return to the first position.

Both bring the hilt to the mouth, the point of the thumb level with the lower lip, sword upright, and edge to the left. This is called "Recover swords." Then turning the face and directing the eyes to the left, slowly and gracefully extend the arm and the sword in the same direction until the point is level with the centre of the face and arm nearly straight, hand in *quarte*, and as high as the shoulder.

After a short pause both again recover swords, and, turning the face to the right, extend the hand in a similar manner to the right. Hand in *tierce*.

From there they recover swords, and, falling on guard, beat a double attack with the right foot (a beat with the heel and one with the flat of the foot in rapid succession). Then, bringing the left foot up to the right, recover swords, and lower the hand and sword slowly towards the right hip. Arm straight, palm down, and edge to the right.

Rules.

You must not attack until an engagement has been formed.

Touches on any part are counted good.

You must not hit after you are touched, but recover to the first position and acknowledge the hit.

After each hit, both men should go to their original ground, and form a fresh engagement before renewing the assault.

When a man leads off with proper quickness, the other should guard before returning. Should he not do so, the hit belongs to the one who led off.

When two men lead off together and both hit, neither hit is counted.

When the *Remise* or Redouble and Return are made together, the hit belongs to the one making the Return.

If the Stop Thrust is not made in sufficient time to prevent the attack being delivered, the hit counts to the one making the attack.

A hit is counted good after a disarmament, if given immediately after and before there is time to think.

Dress for Sabre Play.

Although the figures in the preceding illustrations are shown without masks or pads, no practice ought ever to be made without them. The following is the dress usually worn.

A flannel shirt and trousers, shoes with soles of buff leather, without heels.

A stout leather jacket, arm guard, leather apron, leg guard on right leg, and a pair of shoulder pads, shaped like a milkman's yoke.

A strong helmet covered with leather on the top, with large ear guards, and the mask of strong wire with the meshes sufficiently small to prevent the point of the sabre passing through. A leather stock should also be worn round the neck.

When practising with sticks, the shoulder pad and arm guard may be dispensed with, and the hand ought to be protected with a buffalo hide hand guard.

Basket hilts are dangerous, as the point of the stick is apt to pass through them, and your hand may thereby be seriously injured.

Practice Sabre.

The practice sabre should have a quill edge, which is the bluntest edge there is, and the point should be rounded off.

Sabre v. Bayonet

While writing on this subject, the fencing names of the parries will be used, *viz.*:—

Prime (Head Guard).
Seconde (Outside Leg Guard).
Tierce (Outside Guard).
Quarte (Inside Guard)

In describing how to deal with a man armed with a rifle and bayonet, it will be necessary to explain his methods of attack and defence.

A bayonet should be used like a foil, but in consequence of its weight and general unwieldiness, the simple movements of the latter weapon can only be executed by it, and as the sabre, from its weight and shape, is similarly circumstanced, the two arms, in that respect, are on equal terms.

Plate 21

Engaging Guard.

A bayoneteer, therefore, engages in *tierce* or *quarte*, from which he can make the following attacks:—

A straight thrust.
A disengagement.
Feint a straight thrust and disengage.
"One, Two" (feint a disengagement into one line and disengage into another).

How to Parry his Straight Thrusts and Disengagements.

All his straight thrusts or disengagements over your blade may be parried with *prime*, and all those under your blade with *seconde*.

These parries are stronger than *tierce* and *quarte*, and are, therefore, better adapted for parrying such a heavy weapon as a rifle and bayonet.

They also defend the head and leg as well as the body, while the others only guard the breast.

Tierce and *quarte* may, however, be occasionally used against his thrusts at the breast. A greater variety of returns would be thereby obtained.

How to Parry, "Feint a Straight Thrust, and Disengage."

His feint of a straight thrust, when engaged under the blade and disengagement over the blade, may be parried with *seconde* and *prime*.

His feint of a straight thrust, when engaged over the blade and disengagement under the blade, may be parried with *prime* and *seconde*.

How To Parry "One, Two."

His "One, Two" below and above your blade may be parried with *seconde* and *prime*, and his "One, Two" above and below your blade with *prime* and *seconde*.

If he should deceive your *quarte* by feinting in *quarte* and thrusting in *tierce*, parry *tierce*.

If he deceive your *tierce* by "One, Two," parry *seconde*.

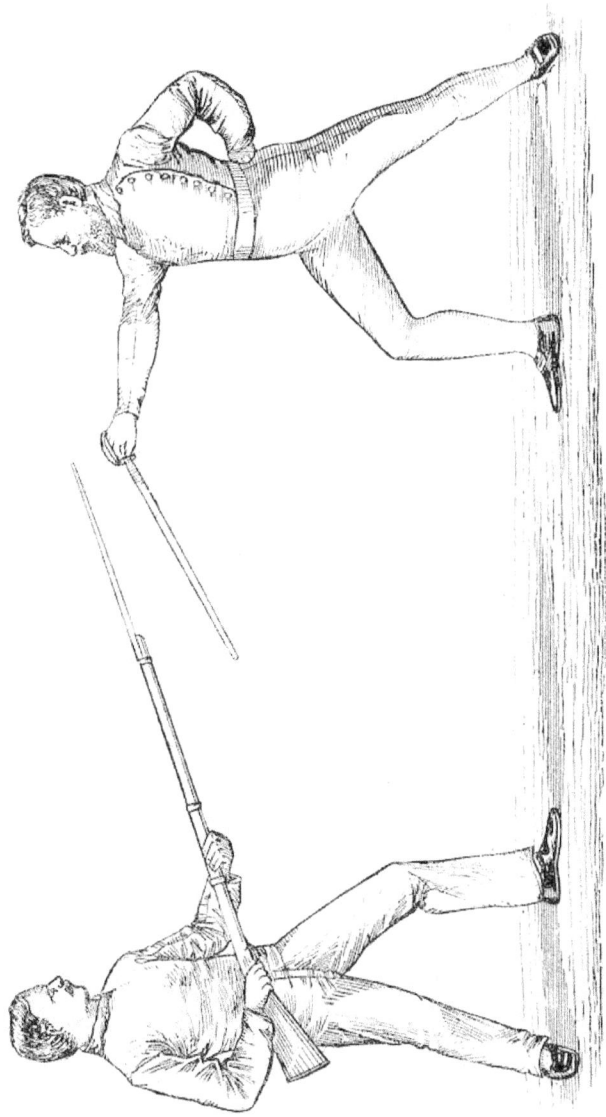

PLATE 21.—ENGAGING GUARD.

Should you at any time foresee that he is going to attack with "One, Two," do not answer the feint, but wait and parry his last movement.

Your parries, which should be made with the edge of the of the sword, must be close, and finished with firmness, without stiffness or too much force.

Returns.

The best returns from the different parries are the following, placed in the order of their comparative merits; but their application should greatly depend on the adversary's defence.

From Parrying *Prime*.

Straight thrust at breast (hand in *tierce* and opposite your right shoulder).

Cut at the left forearm.

Do. head (left diagonal).

Do. inside leg.

From *Seconde*.

Thrust at breast over the guard (palm turned down).

Cut at the right side of the head, neck, or shoulder.

Do. left forearm.

Do. outside leg.

Do. inside leg.

PLATE 22
PARRY OF *TIERCE.*
FROM *TIERCE.*

Thrust at breast under the guard (hand in *tierce* and opposite your right shoulder).

Cut at outside right forearm

Do. head (left horizontal).

Do. head (right diagonal).

Do. inside leg.

PLATE 22.—PARRY OF TIERCE.

PLATE 23
PARRY OF *QUARTE*.
FROM *QUARTE*.

Thrust under left arm (hand in *quarte* and opposite left shoulder).
Cut at the left forearm.
Do. head (right horizontal).
Do. head (left diagonal).
Do. outside leg.

HOW TO ATTACK A MAN ARMED WITH A RIFLE AND BAYONET.

A man thus armed engages in *quarte* or *tierce*, but standing with his left foot in front, his *quarte* will be your *tierce* and his *tierce* your *quarte*; that is, his right side is his *quarte* and your right side is your *tierce*, and *vice versâ*.

He will parry attacks made at the right side of his head or body with *quarte*, and those made at the left side of the head or body with *tierce*.

He will defend the top of his head with *prime* and his leg with half-circle. In both of these guards his left arm is very much exposed.

The following attacks without a feint may be made:—

Cut at his left wrist.

Thrust straight when the line in which he is engaged is not closed.

Disengage with a thrust either from *tierce* to *quarte* or from *quarte* to *tierce*.

PLATE 23.—PARRY OF QUARTE.

PLATE 24

To Deceive his *Prime*.

Feint at head and thrust under his guard. (Hand in *tierce* and opposite your right shoulder.)

Ditto, and cut inside his left wrist (*vide* Plate 24).

Ditto, *ditto*, inside his leg.

PLATE 24.—CUT INSIDE OF WRIST AFTER FEINT AT HEAD TO DECEIVE PRIME.

PLATE 25

To Deceive his Half-Circle.

Feint at inside of leg, and thrust at left breast over the guard. (Hand in *quarte* and opposite your left shoulder.)

Ditto, and cut at his head (*vide* Plate 25.).

Ditto, *ditto*, at his left wrist.

Plate 25—Cut at Head After Feint at Inside Leg to Deceive Half-Circle.

PLATE 26

To Deceive his *Tierce*.

Feint a thrust in *tierce* (his left breast) and disengage with a thrust into *quarte* "One, Two." (Hand in *tierce* and opposite your right shoulder, *vide* Plate 26).

Feint a cut at his left side and cut at his right.

Ditto, ditto, at his left cheek and cut at his right.

Plate 26.—Thrust in *Quarte* after Feint in *Tierce*. "One, Two" to Deceive *Tierce*.

PLATE 27

TO DECEIVE HIS *QUARTE*.

Feint a thrust in *quarte* (his right breast) and disengage with a thrust in *tierce* "One, Two." (Hand in *quarte* and opposite your left shoulder.)

Feint a thrust in *quarte*, and disengage under his left arm "One, Two, Low." (Hand in *quarte* and opposite your left shoulder, *vide* Plate 27).

Feint a cut at his right side and cut at his left arm.

Ditto at his right cheek and cut at his left.

All the above-named attacks may be preceded by a beat or an advance and beat.

The stop thrusts, time thrusts with opposition, *remise*, redouble, and *reprise* can be made upon you by a man armed with a gun and bayonet, and you can use them against him under the same circumstances as when opposed to a sabre.

To avoid his stop thrusts, you must adopt the methods recommended when opposed to a man who engages in *tierce* or *quarte* as described earlier.

PLATE 27.—THRUST UNDER LEFT ARM AFTER FEINT IN *QUARTE* TO DECEIVE *QUARTE*.

GENERAL OBSERVATIONS.

The bayoneteer has the longer weapon. You have the handier one. You must therefore use such tactics as will give it the advantage.

On taking guard, keep out of distance, and by feinting, endeavour to find out whether, if you attack him, he will parry or counter with a thrust, which some men, relying on the superior length of the rifle and bayonet, do when attacked.

If you think that the latter is his intention, make false attacks, as described earlier in 'Drawing', and draw out his thrust, which, having guarded, return with the greatest rapidity. A counter with a bayonet must be avoided by every means possible.

Should you see that he is disposed to guard, you may attack him without much fear of a counter.

You should not attack too often, but rely more upon your guard and quick return. When, however, you do attack, use the feints very much. Doing so gives the advantage to the handier weapon.

Your returns, in which the thrust should take a prominent part, must be made with the greatest rapidity, and the opposition in them, as in the attacks, strictly maintained, so that he cannot possibly deliver a *remise* thrust.

PLATE 28.—HOW TO SEIZE THE RIFLE AFTER PARRYING *PRIME*.

Plate 28

If you at any time have an opportunity of parrying his thrusts with your left hand, or of seizing the barrel of his rifle with it, do so. You must not then struggle and try to get it out of his hands, but must deliver a cut or thrust as quickly as possible. In an actual combat you would then have little difficulty in getting his weapon should you want it.

A good time to attempt this is when, after you have parried *prime*, he does not recover quickly to his guard. You should then step forward quickly with the left foot, and, seizing the rifle, pull it down and towards you, so that he cannot reverse it to strike you with the butt.

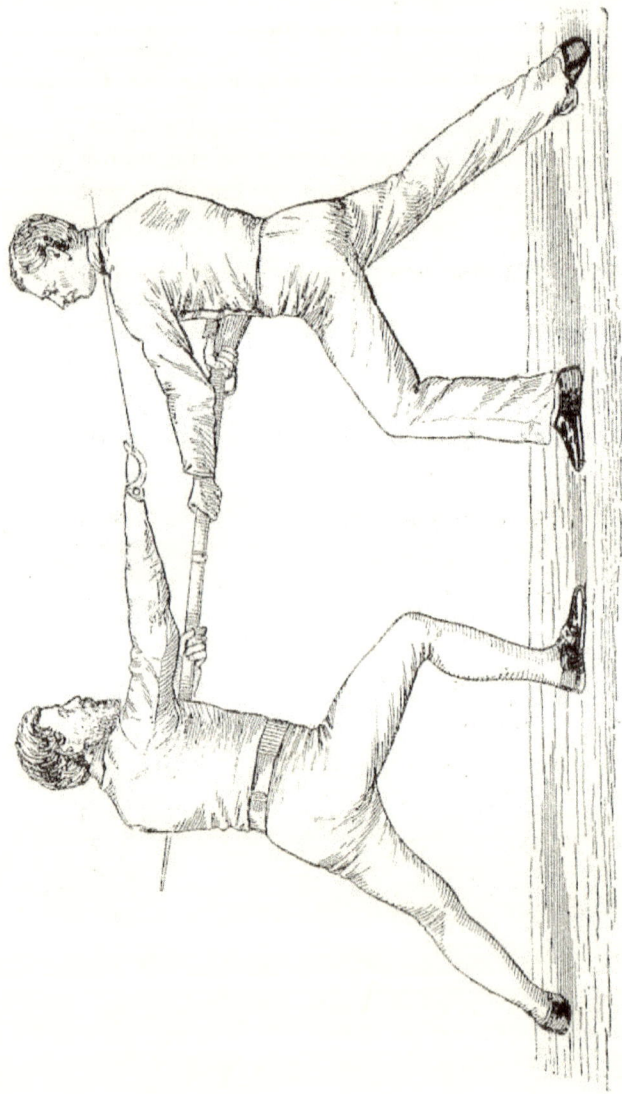

PLATE 29.—How to Seize the Rifle after Parrying Quarte.

PLATE 29

How to Seize the Rifle after Parrying Quarte.

Or you may sometimes get hold of it after your parry of *quarte*, when he is slow in recovering. It will not then be necessary to step forward with the left foot, as your parry will almost send his weapon into your left hand.

Some men when thrusting leave go of the rifle with the left hand. When your adversary does this and you get hold of it, a quick and sudden pull will draw it out of his other hand, or perhaps pull him on his knees.

Dress.

The dress should be the same as that worn when practising with sabres, except that the man using the bayonet should have the pad on his left leg, and both should wear a well-padded fencing or boxing glove on each hand.

On Swords.

It will be useless for me to say anything about the length and shape of swords, as in the British, and, I believe, every other service, an officer, whether he belong to the army, the navy, or the reserve forces, is compelled to wear the regulation sword of the corps he belongs to.

He can, however, purchase it where he likes, and has a certain amount of discretion in small matters, which, if carefully attended to, may make a most important difference in the utility of his weapon. "Mony a mickle mak' a muckle."

I would advise him by all means to get it from a good sword cutler, and see the blade properly proved—a very necessary precaution, as no bad blade will stand so severe a test.

He may then be sure that there is no flaw in it or in the tang (the part that passes through the grip).

A flaw in either may cost you your life.

The blade should be stiff and not whippy, as a whippy blade meets with so much resistance from the air when cutting or guarding quickly, and the point should be light, so that the sword will feel well balanced in the hand.

A whippy blade with a heavy point wrenches the wrist and elbow joints, and is extremely difficult to use. It altogether mars the proper use of the weapon.

The grip should suit your hand, and the steel back should be roughened to prevent the sword from turning in it.

On service, the grip, if not too thick, may be lapped with thin string slightly waxed; by this means it may be altered to any shape you like, and you will be able to hold the sword more securely.

The sword should be tightly mounted, that is, the grip should not be loose, the blade well shouldered up both back and front, so that there is no space between the shoulder and the hilt, and the end of the tang securely screwed and rivetted at the pommel.

To test the mounting, strike both the back and edge of the blade several times sharply against a post. If the grip then remains firm and tight and the blade rings, it is a proof that the mounting is fairly good. Should it, after being used some time, become loose, have it put right at once.

You cannot give an effective cut with a loose-mounted sword. It stings your hand, and spoils the general handling of the weapon.

Scabbard.

The scabbard should be lined with leather or laths of wood, and the mouthpiece with German silver, which is softer than steel, to preserve the edge when drawing and returning the sword.

Edge.

Various edges are put on swords, but the best and most serviceable one, in my opinion, is a short chopper edge. It is the one put on swords used for cutting bars of lead, carcases of sheep and legs of mutton.

The bone of a leg of mutton, which is almost as hard as any substance the edge is likely to come in contact with, will not turn it.

I have now swords with this edge in my possession with which hundreds of bars of lead, numerous carcases of sheep and legs of mutton and other substances have been cut, and the edges are still in good condition and fit for use.

Some Remarks Concerning Sword Hilts.

The shape of the grip in the regulation infantry sword is not bad generally, but the metal back is unnecessary, and is apt to cause the hand to slip.

The grip of Japanese swords, but for the fact of their having the curve presented the wrong way, strikes me as exceedingly good.

Were I having a fighting sword made to my own fancy, without regard to the regulation of any service, I should direct it to be made with a grip of shark's skin or leather, with a strong twist of wire wound round at half-inch intervals, as in the regulation pattern, but continued all the way round without any metal back.

The pommel should be considerably heavier than is customary, and the shell (and I consider this the most important thing) should be of a pattern differing materially from that in common use.

The present form of shell is carried out into a tolerably bold curve on the outer side, no doubt for the purpose of covering the knuckles and arm, which, in a right-handed man, are exposed on this side, while on the reverse side the shell does not project to quite half the same extent.

The consequence of this arrangement is that the greater weight on the outside tends to throw over, I mean, to make the wrist rotate from left to right as it does in attacks on the inner line, and to make rotation correspondingly difficult on the outer line, that is, from right to left.

Now, it may be regarded as proved that attacks on the inner line, although very effective, expose the swordsman more than those delivered at the outside of his adversary's body, consequently the tendency to which I have referred cannot but be considered a vicious one. Again, it may happen that the swordsman is disabled by a flesh wound sufficiently grave to incapacitate his sword arm, but not of such severity as to prevent his continuing in action should he have learned to use his left. If he then pass his sword into his left hand, he will find that the shell, as at present formed, offers a most inadequate protection to the hand and arm, which would not be the case if the projections were equal on both sides.

The Scotch basket hilt, with some modifications, so as to give freer play to hand and wrist, is not a bad pattern.

There should be little or no open work about the shell: an unlucky thrust or cut with the point might disable your hand.

I would also recommend that that part of the shell which comes into contact with the point of the thumb where it rests on the back of the grip should be lightly padded with a few thicknesses of soft leather, so as to lessen the concussion, which is sometimes of sufficient force to loosen your hold of the sword grip, or at all events to impair that nicety of touch upon which successful swordsmanship in a high degree depends.

Before leaving this subject, I should like to remark that, although the grip of the regulation sword is not so faulty as its shell, yet it appears to me capable of improvement.

The back of the grip is convex throughout its length, an arrangement which, when the thumb is pressed upon it, as it should be in the use of a light sabre, does not give so good a hold as one presenting in the lower part a concavity into which shall fit the convex surface of the extended thumb. I have in my possession a pair of practice sabres made upon this principle, and also with a squarer grip than is customary, which are delightful to handle.

Rules of Duelling with Sabres

The Following are the Rules of Duelling With Sabres, Translated from "Essai Sur Le Duel," By The Comte De Chateauvillard.

CHAPTER 7

DUEL WITH SABRES.

1st.—Each combatant must have two seconds for this sort of duel, and one of the two must have a sabre. They must, if possible, get sabres with curved blades for the two antagonists, as being less fatal.

2nd.—When arrived on the ground there must be no discussion between the two combatants, their seconds being their plenipotentiaries.

3rd.—The seconds having agreed upon the choice of the ground the most proper for the combat—level and equal for the two opponents—must mark the two places, the distance being calculated as if the two opponents were both on the *longe* and the points of the two sabres one foot apart.

4th.—The seconds, after having tossed for the places, take their principals to the place given to each by chance.

5th.—Gloves with gauntlets are generally used for this duel, but the seconds of the insulted party (if belonging to the class spoken of in the 11th sec. of the 1st chap.) can oblige the combatants not to wear them. Nevertheless, everyone is entitled to wear an ordinary glove, or a pocket-handkerchief round the hand, but the handkerchief must not hang down.

6th.—If the insulted party (if belonging to the class spoken of in the 10th and 11th secs. of the 1st chap.) wishes to wear a glove with a gauntlet, his seconds must offer a similar one to his opponent, and if the latter refuses it, the insulted party may use his and the other wear an ordinary glove or handkerchief.

7th.—When the combatants are placed, the seconds measure the blades, which must be of equal length and similar shape. The choice of the sabre, if similar ones are used, must be tossed for. If by carelessness the sabres are not alike, the choice should still be tossed for; but if the sabres are too disproportioned for such a combat it should certainly be put off.

8th.—But, however, if the combatants belong to the same regiment they can use their own sabres, but the sabres must be mounted the same.

9th.—The insulted party (if in the class of 11th sec., 1st chap.) can use a sabre belonging to him, but he must offer a similar one to his adversary, who can refuse it and then use his own; nevertheless, if the difference should give a too great disadvantage to either one or the other the seconds should postpone the duel, unless the seconds of both parties present a pair of sabres unknown to the combatants. Then the choice of the pair should belong to the insulted party, and the choice of the sabre to the other.

10th.—The seconds, after having invited the combatants to take off their coats and waistcoats, must go up to their principal's opponent, who must show his naked breast in order to prove that he wears nothing to protect himself against the edge or point of the sabre blade. His refusal would be equivalent to a refusal to fight.

11th.—When what is above described is finished, the seconds should toss for which one of them is to explain the conventions of the duel to the combatants, to whom the weapons are then given, with the recommendation to wait until the signal is given to begin.

12th.—When the seconds are placed on both sides of the combatants, the one designed gives the signal by the word—*Allez!*

13th.—If before the signal is given the combatants join blades together it is equivalent to a signal, but it is blameable if only one of the two does it.

14th.—When the signal is given the combatants can cut and thrust at one another, advance, retire, stoop, turn round, vault, and do anything they think profitable to them: such are the rules of the combat.

15th.—It is against the rules of this combat to strike your opponent when he is disarmed or when he is on the ground, to take hold of his arms or his body or to take hold of his weapon.

16th.—Disarmed means when the sabre has fallen out of the hand, or when dropping the point has touched the ground.

17th.—When one of the combatants is wounded his seconds must stop the combat until they think it proper that it should begin again.

18th.—If before there is any wound one of the seconds wishes to stop the duel, he asks if he can do so to the opposing seconds by lifting up his stick or sabre, and if an affirmative answer is given by the same movement he suspends the duel.

19th.—The seconds can agree beforehand to stop the duel at the first blood shed—humanity and the gravity of the case must guide them.

20th.—If one of the two combatants is killed or wounded against the rules of the duel, the seconds must refer to the 20th and 21st art. of the 4th chap.

DUEL WITH SABRES WITHOUT THRUSTS.

1st.—If possible sabres with blunt points must be used for this duel.

2nd.—Each combatant must have two seconds.

3rd.—The seconds, after having agreed upon the choice of the ground best fitted for the combat—level and equal for the two opponents—must mark the two places at the distance calculated as if the opponents were both on the *longe* and the points joining together.

4th.—Either combatant can use gloves with gauntlets provided the adversary has one too, or that a similar one can be offered to him, otherwise the difference must be levelled by the seconds.

5th.—The weapons must be alike and unknown to the combatants, but if the combatants belong to the same regiment they can use their own sabres, provided they are of the same sort and have the same mountings.

6th.—The seconds, after having tossed for the places, take their friends to the places which have fallen to them.

7th.—The seconds must toss for which of the two antagonists is to choose his sabre.

8th.—The second designed to give the signal must explain to the combatants the conventions of the duel, which are, that it is strictly forbidden to make use of the points of the sabres, which would be felony.

9th.—The seconds invite their friend to strip naked down to the waist, but they may keep their braces on if they are used to them.

10th.—The seconds present both sabres to the combatant who has gained by toss the right to choose, who picks one out, they then present the last one to the other combatant and recommend them both to wait for the signal.

11th.—When the seconds are placed on both sides of the combatants the signal is given by the word—*Allez!*

12th.—When the signal is given the combatants can cut at one another—taking care not to wound their adversary with the point of their sabre—can stoop, advance, retire, turn round, vault, &c., and stop only when the seconds tell them to: such are the rules of the combat.

13th.—The seconds must always stop the duel as soon as one of the combatants is wounded, in order to see whether he can continue or not—the seconds are the only judges for that; but the custom in this kind of duel is to stop the combat at the first wound.

14th.—If one of the combatants is killed or wounded against the rules, *see* 20th and 21st art. of 4th chapter.

Chapters 1st–10th.—The insulted party has the choice of the duel and weapons.

11th.—The insulted party, if struck or wounded, has the choice of the duel, weapons, distances, and can forbid his opponent to use weapons belonging to him, but in that case he must not use his own.

Chapters 4th–20th.—The seconds must, if anything takes place against the rules, make a written statement of it and prosecute the felon by all the laws in their power (and *poursuivre le fauteur devant les tribunaux par toutes les voies de droit en leur pouvoir*).

21st.—The seconds of the party who is charged with felony must, by all means, declare the truth. They are not otherwise accountable for it, unless they aided in committing the wrong, which cannot be supposed possible.

Foil Practice

By George Chapman

EXTRACT

From a Letter Received from Major-General the Hon. Sir J.Yorke Scarlett, K.C.B., Adjutant-General, &c. &c. &c.

The Adjutant-General of the Forces has submitted this Work to his Royal Highness the Duke of Cambridge, Commanding-in-Chief and received the sanction of his Royal Highness to recommend it to the notice of the Officers and non-commissioned Officers of the Army, who may take an interest in the Art of Fencing.

Horse Guards, 3rd Dec. 1860.

A REVIEW OF THE ART OF FENCING

INTRODUCTION

The Art of Fencing is practised in most countries throughout Europe upon the system established in France, and the terms employed in the practice of the foil are either French or derived from the French language. Any one, therefore, desirous of obtaining a thorough knowledge of swordmanship, or professing to teach the art of fencing should make himself conversant with the system adopted in the French School. He may then, in instructing others, impart either the whole or a portion of that system, as may best suit the pupil's convenience, for when time is limited the instructor's endeavour should be to abbreviate the elementary tuition, and to select from the various movements commonly taught in the use of the foil those actions which may be most advantageous to the fencer, sword in hand. Yet, to whatever extent the actual play may be reduced, all fencers should be instructed in the ordinary terms of the art, and be made to understand the scheme

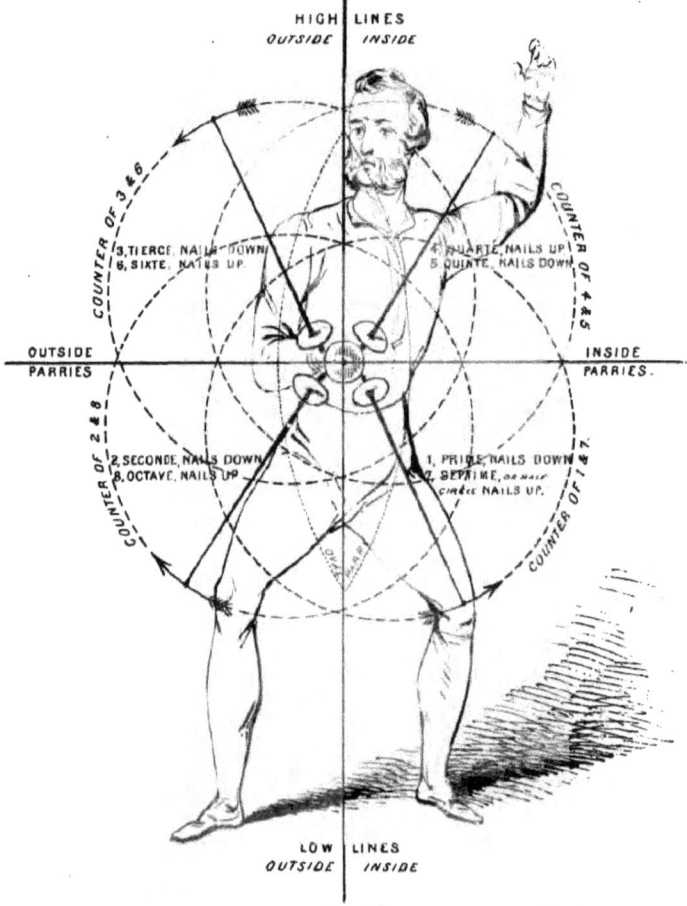

A DIAGRAM

OF THE PARRIES OF THE FOIL

OR

PLAN UPON WHICH THE SYSTEM OF DEFENCE IS FOUNDED

HIGH LINES
OUTSIDE   INSIDE

COUNTER OF 3 & 6

COUNTER OF 4 & 5

3, TIERCE, NAILS DOWN
6, SIXTE, NAILS UP.

4, QUARTE, NAILS UP
5, QUINTE, NAILS DOWN

OUTSIDE
PARRIES

INSIDE
PARRIES.

COUNTER OF 2 & 8

COUNTER OF 1 & 7

2, SECONDE, NAILS DOWN
8, OCTAVE, NAILS UP.

1, PRIME, NAILS DOWN
7, SEPTIME, or half circle, NAILS UP.

LOW LINES
OUTSIDE   INSIDE

FOR THE DEVIATIONS OF THE HAND FROM THE CENTRE
& MORE PRECISE POSITIONS OF THE PARRIES, SEE PLATE PAGE 14.

STANNARD & DIXON.

upon which the recognised method of attack and defence is founded. To assist in rendering that information is the chief object of this work.

Part the First of the following pages contains, with plates and a diagram of the parries of the foil, a brief explanation of the French system of fencing; and Part the Second a few instructions selected from that system, as best adapted for facilitating the practice of the foil.

PART 1.

All attacks are, in the direction of their delivery, consequent upon the mode of defence opposed to them. The manner in which an antagonist places himself on guard, and the methods he employs in forming his parries, prompt us in choosing a point of attack, and control us in the guidance of our weapon. It is, therefore, advisable, in studying the art of fencing, to commence with an examination of the scheme of defence. By so doing even those who are unacquainted with the art will more easily comprehend the whole system of fencing when they come to investigate the plan of attack.

THE DEFENCE.

Now a swordsman presenting his point to the front, either defensively or offensively, may be himself attacked in any one of the following four directions, termed the lines of defence:—

On the left of his swordhand beneath the hilt. The low line inside
On the right, beneath the hilt. The low line outside.
On the right, above the hilt. The high line outside.
On the left, above the hilt. The high line inside.

It will thus be seen that, with a sword of ordinary length, one only of these lines can be defended at a time, and, consequently, the three other lines must remain open to the adversary's attack. (The lines of defence moving with and being determined by the position of the hilt, and not exactly by imaginary divisions on the body.)

For the defence of each line there are two parries (see diagram), the sword in both parries being placed in a similar direction, the parries themselves differing only in the position of the sword's edge, the sword-hand being held in the one case in supination (the nails turned upwards), and in the other in pronation (the nails turned downwards).

These eight parries, sometimes called parades, are denominated by French numerical appellations, derived from the Latin, *viz*.: 1. *Prime*; 2. *Seconde*; 3. *Tierce*; 4. *Quarte*; 5. *Quinte*; 6. *Sixte*; 7. *Septime* (commonly called Half-circle); and 8. *Octave*.

Fencing masters have differed, and some still differ, in the numerical arrangement of the parries; but the following allotment for the defence of each line is, at the present day, generally recognised, and, although in their numerical order the parries may appear slightly misplaced, custom compels their adoption as follows. From the centre of the right breast and with the elbow moderately bent, the thumb pressed along the convex or upper side of the grip in direct line with the point:

1.—Prime and 7.—Half-circle	The hand tending to the left, the point lowered and inclined to the left, the finger-nails turned down. The same, but with the nails turned up and the arm elongated.	Parry the attack directed on the inside low
2.—Seconde and 8.—Octave	The hand tending to the right, the arm straightened, the point lowered and inclined to the right, the finger nails turned down. The same, but with the nails turned up.	Parry the attack directed on the outside low
3.—Tierce and 6.—Sixte	The hand tending to the right, the point raised and inclined to the right, the finger-nails turned down. The same, but with the nails turned up.	Parry the attack directed on the outside high
4.—Quarte 5.—Quinte.	The hand tending to the left, the point raised and inclined to the left, the finger-nails turned up (slightly). The same, but with finger nails turned down.	Parry the attack directed on the inside high

The defence is thus varied by the turn of the wrist, in the same lines, for the purpose of exercising a greater or a less amount of resistance upon the adversary's blade, and for facilitating and regulating, in accordance with the position of supination or of pronation, the attack in return immediately after having parried (termed the Repost). The direction of the finger-nails is also regulated in accordance with the description of sword employed, that is, whether of the triangular or two-edged construction, so as to avoid the error of parrying with the flat of the blade,.

A proper application of the edge in warding either a cut or a thrust is thus acquired in practising with a quadrangular blade or foil (mounted, as the sword-blade is, with pummel handle and hilt), and from its pliancy better suited for practice than the actual small sword (the weapon which the foil is more particularly intended to represent). The small sword is of the triangular shape, hollowed between each edge, and so mounted that when properly held, one edge is presented to the ground, one to the right, and one to the left. The parries are, however, so contrived that they may be performed with either a two or a three-edged sword, and are effected with the *forte* of the blade (or the half near the hilt), and either by a sharp close beat or by a simple resistance upon the adversary's *foible*. (Of the blade from the middle to the point.)

In forming the engagement (*i.e.*, crossing the adversary's blade), and in parrying, the elbow of the sword-arm is in most cases moderately bent, the thumb of the sword-hand pressed on the upper side of the grip (handle), upon the inner side of which the fingers are regularly placed. They should in no case be lapped over the convex or upper side, as by so doing the necessary play with the handle would be lost to the hand. In the engagement the sword should be held securely, but without any strain upon the hand, the fingers tightening their hold at the moment the blades are joined in the junction of the parry.

In making use of any one of the parries, there are two methods of throwing off the adversary's blade; *viz.*, either by throwing it off in the same line or division in which it is directed, or by throwing it off in an *opposite* line or division from that in which it is directed; and the parries are expressed according to the manner in which they are performed, under the terms of simple parries, counters, and semi-counters.

SIMPLE PARRIES.

The position of each parry is also a position of defence (engagement) adopted upon crossing swords with an adversary, thus obliging him to direct his attack into another line (to disengage), and the parries are termed simple parries; when, in parrying the adversary's disengagement, the position of defence is changed, and the point is passed in *direct* course from one side to the other, either in the high or the low lines, for example, from *tierce* to *quarte*, *quarte* to *tierce* (high lines); *septime* to *seconde*, *seconde* to *septime* (low lines); or when the point is raised and lowered from the high to the low, or from the low to the high lines on the *same* side, that is, for example, from *quarte* to *septime*, *septime* to *quarte*, or from *tierce* to *seconde*, and *seconde* to *tierce*. Thus, the simple parries always throw off the attack in the line in which it is directed.

COUNTERS.

The parries are termed counters (meaning in opposition to) when the sword-hand (in parrying a disengagement) retains the line of defence, describing with the point a circular course round the adversary's blade until it meets it again in the line from which it first proceeded (the original engagement), throwing off the attack in an *opposite* line from that in which it is directed.

This circular movement, performed by the action of the fingers more than by that of the wrist, commences *under* the adversary's blade in the *high* lines, and over his blade in the *low*; thus, for example, from the engagement of *quarte*, upon the adversary's disengagement, the circle is described by lowering the point, passing it under his blade, towards the right, returning upwards and resuming the position of *quarte*. From the engagement in the other lines the disengagements are parried upon the same principle, *the arrowheads in the diagram denoting the course taken by the foil.* The counter action is also performed upon the adversary's direct thrust in the line of defence, when the line is not properly secured. Thus, for example, in the line of *quarte*, the direct thrust is parried by dropping the point under the adversary's blade and circling upwards, throwing off the attack in the opposite line (that of *tierce*), and upon the direct thrust in the line of *tierce*, by a similar action throwing off the attack in the opposite line (that of *quarte*).

This action in parrying is by some teachers denominated the half-counter; but as the point in the parry describes a full circle, other masters reasonably object to the application of the term, excepting as follows:

Semi-Counters.

The parries are termed semi-counters, when by a half-circular action, (or traverse action), the attack is thrown off from a high line into the *opposite* low (that is, for example, from *quarte* to *seconde*), or brought upwards from a low line into the *opposite* high (that is, for example, from *septime* to *tierce*). Thus, the semi-counters, like the counters, always throw off the attack in an opposite line from that in which it is directed. It will therefore be observed, that in performing the simple parries the hand must be moved from one line of defence to another, but that in executing the counter-parries the hand should be maintained in its position, as a pivot, upon which the point revolves.

When in performing the circular movement the adversary's blade is parried in an adverse sense to that prescribed by rule, or by a binding effort dragged into the opposite lines, or carried round again into the line where first met with, the action is termed a parry of *contraction*. This mode of parrying is by many fencing-masters condemned as irregular. In all quick fencing, however, contraction in parrying occasionally and unavoidably occurs, and although it should be avoided as a rule, yet expert fencers at times purposely employ the method, to check abruptly the play of complicated attacks. There are other somewhat objectionable manners of effecting the parries, one of which consists in parrying (*quarte* and *sixte*) with a flying point, as it is termed. That is in lifting the point vertically (or towards the shoulder) and with a backward action whipping the adversary's blade out of line. Some fencers also perform the parries of *quarte* and *tierce* by whipping the blade, with a forward action, along that of the adversary's. Both these methods, although not generally approved of, may be, however, occasionally permitted.

As a *general* parry, a circular or deep elliptic movement of the point directly in front of the body, from right to left, or left to right (the hilt maintained at the centre, and the sword passing rapidly through each line of defence) may be adopted (see dotted lines). This system of defence is sometimes employed with much success.

In like manner any one of the counter-parries may be described with the point, in oval as well as circular form, and any one of the simple parries, slightly altered by vertical or horizontal tendencies given to the blade.

All these parries are performed, standing firm, on the advance or in the retreat, and may be, upon occasions, more or less diverted in angle, altitude, and circumference from the centre, or positions marked in the diagram, the diagram being merely intended to show at a glance the lines of defence, and to afford an insight into the principles upon which the parries are founded.

Prime, for example, under the definition " high," is frequently performed above the head, with the elbow bent; and *septime*, as "half-circle high," with the arm nearly straightened, on a level with the shoulder; the hand in both these deviations being carried to the right (or upper line outside), while in *quinte*, (when thus performed this parry is sometimes called low-*quartre*), it is lowered towards the left hip; the point is also generally presented more to the front, or opposite the adversary, forming a lesser angle than appears in the diagram, the circle of the counter reduced (sometimes to a very small compass), in accordance with the closeness of the adversary's disengagement, and the position of the hand modified in the degree of supination or pronation in which it is placed; (the parry of *quarte* being frequently effected with the fingernails but very slightly inclined upwards).

Prime is also occasionally performed, when the direct thrust is de-

ACTUAL POSITIONS OF THE PRINCIPAL PARRIES

TIERCE

COUNTER OF

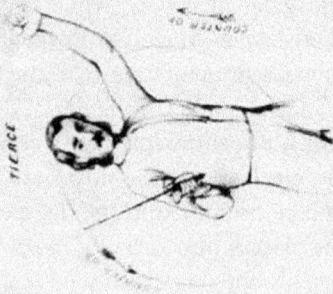

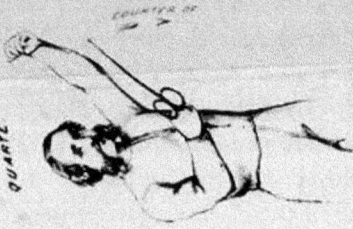

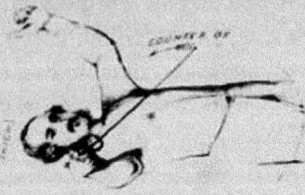

FROM THIS POSITION
Incline the hand towards the right shoulder
& turn up the nails to form
SIXTE

SECONDE

FROM THIS POSITION
Incline the hand slightly to the right
& turn up the nails to form
OCTAVE

QUARTE

COUNTER OF

FROM THIS POSITION
Incline the hand to the left hip,
& turn down the nails to form
QUINTE

SEPTIME or HALFCIRCLE

COUNTER OF

FROM THIS POSITION
Raise the hand above the forehead turn out
the elbow & turn down the nails to form
PRIME (hand)
PRIME & HALFCIRCLE (foil)
are formed the same, as a parry with the wrist
turn the hand inclined to the left

livered in the engagement of *tierce*, by simply yielding the wrist and blade (lowering the point) to the adversary's pressure, and that without quitting his foil. The parry of *quarte* may be likewise maintained by yielding to force, when from the engagement of *quarte,* the blade is encircled by the opponent's foil, and his point presented in the low-line outside. These variations from the centre, together with the actual positions of the principal parries, as they are usually effected, may be better understood upon referring to the subjoined plates.

The combinations of the parries are formed by uniting two or more parries in continuous action, so that the adversary's blade if missed in one line may be met in another; *i.e.*, by performing a simple parry after a counter; or a circular after a simple; or a semi-circular after a circular; or two circular, either in the same or in opposite lines; as, for examples:—

From the engagements upon the adversary's corresponding dis-engagements.

From the engagement of *Quarte—tierce* counter *tierce, quarte,* and counter-*quarte*, termed the opposite counters, when formed in union and by passing the point under the adversary's blade.

From the engagement of *Tierce*, the same, but reversed in order.

From the engagement of *Quarte*—the counter of *quarte*, and simple *tierce*.

From the engagement of *Tierce*—the counter of *tierce* and *quarte*.

From the engagement of *Quarte*—the counter of *quarte*, half-circle, and *quarte* again.

From the engagement of *Tierce*—the counter of *tierce, seconde,* and *tierce* again; or from either engagement half-circle high, the counter of half-circle, and *seconde*.

From the hand held at the centre—*quarte*, counter-*quarte*, half-circle, and *tierce*; or, *tierce*, counter-*tierce*, *seconde*, and *quarte* in continuous action, also form the two counters, or circles in the opposite courses, the point being passed alternately through the lines of defence, and in so doing describing a somewhat deeper figure than usual.

In like manner, from the engagement in any one of the lines of defence, the simple, semi-counter, and counter parries, may be united and varied in their order of succession, but these systematic combinations can only be properly acquired by practice with the foil, and through the personal demonstration of the instructor.

THE ATTACK.

Position—On Guard.

There are but two attitudes assumed and maintained throughout in fencing; *viz.*, the position of defence on guard, and the *longe* on attack. As a preliminary position the fencer may place the heel of the right foot against the left ankle, his left arm resting at his side, his right hand holding the foil pointed downwards over his right knee, his head erect, and turned towards his adversary. From this position the attitude of defence is assumed by the fencer:

1. Raising his sword-hand directly to the front, and bending his elbow until the pummel is opposite the centre of his breast, the point directed towards the opponent's shoulder, on the right or left, according to the line of engagement, *i.e., quarte* or *tierce.*

2. Raising the left arm above his head with the hand inclined towards his face.

3. Bending the knees freely or until they cover the toes: and

4. Advancing the right foot from the left in distance to about two lengths of the fencer's foot. All these movements, when understood, should be performed simultaneously, the head and bust supported in an erect position, the body resting equally on both legs, the chest turned fairly towards the opponent; without the right shoulder being thrown altogether sideways, and without the left shoulder being brought too much to the front, but preserving a just medium of position, so that the hips may be worked equally with the shoulders.

Some fencers place the right heel opposite the left heel when on guard, but with the right heel placed in line with the left ankle the position of attack or *longe* may be more favourably effected.

THE *LONGE* AND RECOVERY

To perform which, the fencer—

1. Straightens his sword-arm until the pummel is on a level with his shoulder; the fingers turned upwards, the hand borne either to the right or to the left, according to the line of engagement, *i.e., quarte or tierce*, the point lowered and directed towards the opponent's breast

2. Lowers the left shoulder and arm, the hand open and the knuckles inclined towards the left knee.

3. Straightens the left leg.

4. Advances the right foot four times the length of the foot, so that the knee may, on the fall of the foot, rest perpendicular to the instep.

These movements, when understood, should be performed together with the greatest rapidity, and with the head and body supported in an erect position throughout; the propulsion being effected in relaxing a previous compression in the muscles of the loins and in the sudden straightening of the left knee. In straightening the arm, the muscles should not be overstretched—an imperceptible bend in the elbow should be retained.

In recovering the position of defence—

1. The left knee is bent.

2. The left arm raised.

3. The right foot replaced upon the point at which it rested previous to the performance of the *longe.*

4. The right elbow again moderately bent, with the sword-point retained opposite the opponent's breast.

In *longeing* and in recovering to the position of defence, the action of raising and lowering the left arm as a balance to the body should not be neglected.

THE ADVANCE.

There are two methods of advancing; the regular and most usual is performed by first advancing the right foot, and then, in due distance, bringing forward the left, the knees throughout being kept bent (or in the same position as when on guard). The advance is, however, occasionally performed by first moving the left foot towards the right.

THE RETREAT

There are three methods of retiring; the regular and most usual is performed by first withdrawing the left foot and then removing, in due measure, the right; the knees being kept bent throughout the action. Retiring is, however, occasionally performed by first withdrawing the right, and then removing the left, and in cases of emergency sometimes effected by springing backwards from both feet simultaneously. The paces are generally more lengthened in the retreat than in the advance.

All these actions, *viz.*: the advance, the retreat, the *longe*, the recovery, and position of defence are performances, in the execution of which the strictest adherence to regularity should be observed; the points mostly to be borne in mind being—In the *longe*—the advance of the sword-hand before that of the foot, the complete straightening of the left knee, the lowering of the left hand, and the perfect hold of the left foot (toe and heel) on the ground. In the recovery—the bend of the left knee, the maintenance of the sword-hand to the front, and the elevation of the left arm; and in both the attack and defence a constant support of the head and bust in an upright position, the weight equally balanced on the centre, and not, according to an old system, thrown on the left leg.

The attack is either premeditated or unpremeditated; conceived and executed instantaneously upon opportunities occurring, or made without regard to what may occur in the defence opposing it, and when success also depends upon quickness and precision only; or commenced with the semblance of an attack (feint), and conducted in its subsequent course according to the adversary's play or parry. For as (from the engagement) the defence is sustained by simple semi-counter and counter-parries, so (from the engagement) the attack is effected by direct thrusts, disengagements and counter-disengagements.

All thrusts, as well as the engagements, are designated under the *nomenclature* of the parries, according to the manner in which the hand is placed, whether of supination or pronation, and the line in which the attack is directed. Thus, it is said, from the engagement of *tierce* disengage and thrust *quarte* in the inside line high, or thrust *sixte* in the outside line high, *octave* in the outside line low, &c. &c. &c.

Upon coming to the engagement (on guard) which generally and naturally (though not of necessity) is taken in one of the high lines (*quarte* or *tierce*, for example); and upon entering within reach of the adversary's point (measure) it is best to regulate, at once, the position of the hilt by that of the adversary's, and to endeavour, in crossing his blade by a gentle pressure with the *forte* of the sword upon his *foible* to close the line of defence.

(The guard may be either partly offensive or wholly defensive. It is offensive when the arm is elongated and the point presented at the adversary. Defensive when, with the elbow bent and the point raised, the fencer's sole intent is to parry.)

This resistance of the sword (opposition), greater or less, according to circumstances, should, upon all occasions, be carefully maintained. It is of the utmost consequence in obtaining an advantage in the engagement, by keeping the opponent's weapon out of line, and also in avoiding the chance of being hit in the act of delivering a hit, *i.e.,* in barring off, by the direction given to the edge, the adversary's point, if in lieu of parrying he thrusts upon a thrust. This touch of the sword, and the faculty of sight together (the eye being chiefly fixed upon the adversary's hilt), regulate the fencer's play.

When the advantage in the engagement is obtained, and consequently the adversary's breast exposed, the attack may be delivered with a direct thrust. When, on the contrary, the adversary commands the advantage of engagement, the attack must be delivered by disengaging (*i.e.,* lowering the point under his hilt, and thrusting in one of the low lines); or by passing the point near and over his hilt into the *opposite* high line; or by passing the point *over his point*, also into the opposite high line (cut over point), carefully observing the opposition in all these movements. In fencing, the term "cut over" does not apply to the use of the edge, but only to the cutting-like actions of the hand and wrist in lowering the pummel and throwing the point over the adversary's point.

The menace of a direct thrust, and disengagements without *longeing*, are practised as feints, to force the adversary to an engagement if he avoids crossings the blade, or to induce him to quit his line of defence, so that in his attempt to parry in one line he may be hit in another.

Most feints may be either performed by a simple turn of the wrist, or effected as the disengagements usually are, *viz.,* with the *foible*, or that portion of the blade used as the offensive (the half near the point) without bending the elbow or withdrawing the arm; and at first by an action of the fingers only (chiefly by pressure and relaxation of the thumb and forefinger), the wrist moving in its turn towards the final delivery of the thrust. The thrust is generally terminated with the point lowered, the hand sustained, and the fingers in supination—tightening their hold on the grip in the course of the action.

All feints, half or whole attacks made at the body, may be preceded by attacks made upon the sword, by beating, wrenching, sliding, binding, or pressing upon the adversary's blade.

Binding or encircling the adversary's blade is a performance also executed in conjunction with the delivery of a thrust, generally from the inner lines into one or the other of the outside lines. Binding the opponent's blade from the engagement of *quarte*, and at the same time delivering a thrust in the low line outside formerly passed under the appellation of *flanconade.*

When the adversary attempts to parry a disengagement by a simple parry, he will be deceived by a second disengagement (one, two). When he attempts to parry a disengagement by a counter parry, he will be deceived by a counter-disengagement, *i.e.,* by a circular advance of the point round his blade in the same course as his counter, until the position of the first disengagement is resumed, and the thrust delivered.

In this manner all combinations of simple and counter-parries are evaded by corresponding combinations of disengagements and counter-disengagements; or arrested in their action by a beat, wrench, or pressure upon the adversary's blade. The parries of contraction are avoided upon the same principle; but when the blade is jarred, or entangled with the adversary's, it is advisable to withdraw the point, and then resume the play.

The direct return thrust (repost) or attack after the parry, when the parry has been properly performed, and has thrown the adversary's blade *out of line*, should be delivered with the greatest rapidity—from the position of the parry—observing the opposition, and—without any other movement but that of the sword-arm. Return thrusts, not direct, are delivered by disengaging, cutting over the point, or passing under the hilt, either without *longeing* or with the *longe*; in the latter case, during the adversary's recovery to the position of defence. Return thrusts are generally executed with the hand in supination, but from the parries of *prime* and *seconde* occasionally with the hand in pronation.

The change of engagement (and double change of engagement) in the high lines is performed in passing the point under the adversary's blade, and by a circular movement joining it again in the opposite line; thus, for example, from the engagement of *tierce* passing under the adversary's blade to the engagement of *quarte*, and in a similar manner from *quarte* to *tierce*. From the engagements in the low lines (from *seconde* to *septime* for example) the change is performed by passing over the *forte* of the adversary's blade into an opposite line. Rapidity of action in changing the engagements is of very great advantage, being an attack on the adversary's blade, and at the same time serving as a defence. It is this constant change of engagement (or dispute for the line of defence) which causes the continual motion of the foil observable in the play of expert fencers.

In changing the engagements, the fencer may be deceived by his adversary disengaging, and therefore while performing any change, feint, or attack, whether on the advance or from the fixed position of the guard, the swordsman should be always ready to parry, or prepared to; resist the delivery of a time thrust.

The time thrust is a sudden attack, usually made with a *longe* upon the adversary's feint, disengagement, change, attack, or preparation for attack; it is designated by the term of a Stop Thrust when it arrests the adversary on his advance, and is called a Certain Time Thrust when performed upon his *longe*, because, to succeed in its execution, a certainly of the line in which the adversary's attack is directed is of absolute necessity, the only dependence for security being in the opposition of the blade. Time thrusts, when well executed, are often skilful performances of swordmanship, but it is necessary to be careful of their employment, as the danger, in their practice, of incurring mutual hits is very great.

In that of the certain time thrust so much so that it is almost always preferable to parry and throw in the repost. Time thrusts may be performed with less risk in the outside fines than in the inside; for example, whenever the adversary passes his point into the outside line high, by *longeing* upon him in the same line with a forced opposition and with the hand in supination, whenever he passes his point into the outside line low, by thrusting upon him in the same line and with the opposition in octave.

Repeating the thrust while upon the *longe* is another method of delivering a time thrust, termed a *remise*. It is repeated width the hand, generally, in supination, though sometimes in pronation, upon the adversary's delay in reposting—or upon wide movements with his point after his parry—or upon his advance to repost after having parried; the *remise* is provoked by opportunities afforded in the adversary's play, and in that respect differs essentially from the *reprise*, a redoubling of the attack, also made while upon the *longe*, but without regard to the adversary's play, and with the premeditated intent of throwing in the point at all hazards.

★★★★★★★★★★

A sudden repetition of attack, *after* recovering to the position of defence, is sometimes termed the *reprise* of attack. When the attack is thus renewed, it does not partake of the objectionable character of the *reprise* while resting upon the *longe*.

★★★★★★★★★★

Repetitions of attacks of this kind, rushing upon or attempting to disarm the adversary, retreating from every attack, the use of the left hand, withdrawing the arm to deliver the thrust, vaulting to the right or left, and the frequent extension of the sword-arm without *longeing*, are practices condemned in fencing by all competent authorities.

It should be remembered that the rules of fencing are formed with a view of rendering the swordsman's play safer to himself when actually engaged with an enemy; no one could with impunity rest upon his *longe*, or rush in stabbing at hazard with an adverse point directed at his face.

Such practices would be dangerous, even when only opposed to the blunted foil, unless protected with the mask. Excellence in fencing is shown by the players preserving due measure, attacking with the *longe*, and recovering the position of defence;—in close parrying—quick reposting, and—regularity and simplicity of play. In the rules of conventional fencing no touch is reckoned unless delivered on the bust—that is, from the neck to the waist, provided that the players do not purposely hide the breast with the sword-arm or by contortions of the body. It is well, however, occasionally to reckon all touches above the hip.

When mutual hits occur, the hit is reckoned in favour of the fencer making the attack, provided the attack does not occupy an unreasonable time in its delivery. When mutual hits occur between the *remise* and the repost the hit is reckoned in favour of the fencer making the repost. No attack should consist of more than two or three consecutive movements. To hit, and not to be hit, is the swordman's object, and therefore the fewer his movements the better; Fencing in all its intricacies resolving itself mainly into the simple facts:

1st. That he who parries has but to meet his adversary's blade by *direct* movements, or by *circling* round it.

2nd. That he who attacks has but to pass his point from one *side to the other* of his adversary's weapon, *to circle within its circle*, or by an attack upon the blade, obtain an opening wherein to thrust.

The combinations of the disengagements consist in uniting the simple and counter-disengagements in continuous action, so that the point may be passed through the adversary's combinations of parries without touching his blade, *i.e.,* to disengage and counter-disengage, upon his simple and counter-parries, or to counter-disengage and disengage upon his counter and simple parries, and to vary the attack in cutting over the point, passing close to the blade or under the hilt; thus, for example, to cut over the adversary's point, to disengage under his hilt, and pass the point upwards into the original line of engagement, is but to form a circle or "turn" around his blade; or to mark one, two, three when he defends himself with the simple parries alone, is but to perform a continuous advance of the point in vertical gradation.

Examples of deceptions of this kind will be found in the following part, but they cannot be properly learned by book alone. To particularise attacks, preceded by a single feint (always the safest), is unnecessary. They are executed by feinting in a low line to thrust in a high, or threatening on one side to thrust on another, or cutting over and disengaging under, or disengaging and cutting over, performed either directly from the engagement, or preceded by a beat or change. Attacks of this description may be as easily conceived by the reader as it is possible to express them in writing.

To attain exactitude in the performance of the disengagements and their combinations, and to obtain a perfect knowledge of the various modes of attack, the personal instructions of the fencing-master are absolutely necessary.

EXAMPLES OF THE REPOSTS AS THEY ARE USUALLY DELIVERED.

From:

Prime, Low.—By raising the point in a circular course (with an inward turn of the hand) towards the left shoulder, and throwing the attack upon the adversary in one or another of the inner lines.

This *repost* may be performed with the addition of a beat, as the blade in its circular course comes into the position of *quarte*, and previous to throwing in the point.

Prime, High.—The same, and also by the direct thrust, with the nails turned down.

Seconde.—By turning the nails up and thrusting with the opposition of *sixte*, in the outside line high; or when the parry has thrown the adversary's blade well out of line, by thrusting (with the nails turned down) in the low-line inside.

Tierce.—By thrusting in the outside lines, high or low (the nails either up or down), but when the adversary rests upon his *longe* the repost can be more easily delivered with the nails turned down.

Quarte.—By the direct thrust in the engagement of *quarte*; or by cutting over the point or disengaging either into the outside line high, or under the adversary's hilt.

Flying *Quarte.*—By passing the point (in continuous and circular action with the parry) over the adversary's point into the low line outside.

Quinte.—By turning up the nails and thrusting in the inside line high; or by passing the point over the adversary's *forte* and thrusting (with the nails turned up) under his hilt into the low line outside.

Sixte.—By thrusting in the outside line low, directly under the adversary's arm. In delivering this *repost* the fencer may assist himself by lowering the body with a slight bend of the knees.

Flying *Sixte.*—By passing the point over the adversary's point in circular and continuous action with the parry, and delivering the thrust in the inside line low. The flying parries of *quarte* and *sixte* are rapid in effect, but are sometimes objected to, because while delivering the *repost* the lines of defence are entirely deserted.

Septime, or Half-circle, Low.—The same as low *prime*, or by disengaging over the adversary's *forte*, or thrusting with the nails turned down, in the low line.

High.—The same as high *prime*, or by thrusting under the adversary's arm in the low line inside, or by encircling his blade and thrusting over his arm in the outside line high.

Octave.—By thrusting with a forced opposition in the outside line low. This *repost* is usually performed simultaneously with the parry, and thus becomes a certain time thrust.

In effecting the parries, the fencer should exert an additional influence over his adversary's blade beyond throwing it aside, by slightly elevating or depressing it, according to the line, high or low, in which it is the intention to deliver the *repost*, and although the parries should be usually performed without retreating (when the adversary does not advance) a short step backwards is occasionally advantageous. In all cases sufficient space should, if possible, be preserved (by advancing or retiring) for the delivery of the *repost* after the parry.

THRUSTING, QUARTE, AND TIERCE.

(Custom has established the term thrusting in *quarte* and *tierce*, but strictly speaking it should be said in *quarte* and *sixte*, the disengagement in the outside line being performed, like that in the inside, with the hand in supination.)

With the manner of saluting (a complimentary form) previous to the assault (or loose play).

The exercise of thrusting in *quarte* and *tierce* is usually connected with the salute, and is generally performed previous to the assault or loose play. By thrusting in *quarte* and *tierce* the fencers prepare themselves for subsequent exertion, and exhibit their capabilities in executing the *longe*, disengagement, parry, and *repost*. The performances, and the exhibition thereof are, in fact, to the fencer what "marching past" is to the soldier. Fencing-masters differ, slightly, in the number and order of the paces, or, as they are termed, "passes" of the feet in the performance of the salute, but it may be thus rightly executed.

Facing each other in the upright position, without wearing their masks, the fencers present the points of their weapons towards each other, turn down the fingernails, lower and pass the point backwards, lay the hilt upon the back of the left hand, the palm of the left hand resting on the left thigh; raise both hands above the head, the left hand retaining its situation under the hilt; fall on guard, crossing swords in the engagement of *quarte*, beat twice with the right foot and expose the full bust the hand in *tierce*). By accordance one of them then takes his distance, *longeing* with the hand and opposition in *quarte*, within reach of, but without touching, his adversary; both rise to the upright position by bringing the right heel to the left; both salute the spectators by turning the sword-hand to *quarte*, to *tierce*, and afterwards the point towards each other, suiting the movement of head and eye to the action of the hand; both again pass, as before, the hilt to the left hand and above the head and fall on guard, in *quarte*.

He who in the first instance *longed* now passes a disengagement with the nails up, into the outside line high, maintains the opposition of the blade, and (by slackening his hold upon the *grip*, and reversing his fingers) turns the point towards himself; the pummel towards his adversary. (The disengagement should be fully developed before the point is reversed.) Thus, directing his glance, under his arm, between his sword-hand and his blade, he rests a moment or two upon his *longe*. Upon this disengagement (which should never be performed until *after* the junction of the blades in the engagement) he on the defence parries *tierce*, and presents his point as in the return of second, but without touching.

The fencer on the attack resumes the position of defence, but now in the engagement of *tierce*; disengages in *quarte*, again reversing the point, in this instance towards his right shoulder, the pummel towards his adversary, the opposition carefully maintained, and the eye directed over the arm between the sword-hand and the blade.

Upon this disengagement he, on the defence, parries *quarte*, and presents his point as in the return of half-circle, but without touching. After a few *longes* in this manner the fencer on the attack beats twice with the foot, marks (from *quarte*) one, two, without *longeing*, and uncovering (with his hand, and point in *tierce*) affords his opponent the

POSITIONS OF THE HAND & HILT.

While resting on the lunge during the performance of
THE SALUTE

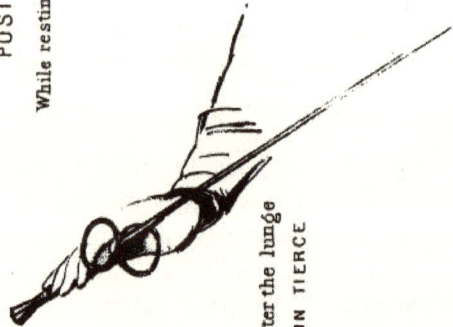

after the lunge.
IN QUARTE

After the lunge
IN TIERCE

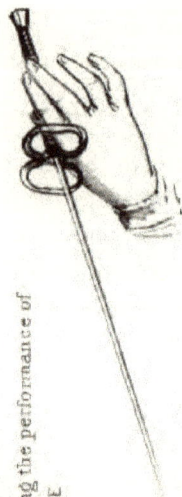

opportunity, in his turn, of *longeing* to take his measure of attack.

★★★★★★★★★★

Some fencers, when offering the opening to the opponent to take his measure of attack, in the first instance, rise to the upright position by bringing the right foot to the left. Others while performing "one, two" in offering the opening upon the second occasion, also assume the upright position, by bringing the left foot to the right, resuming the position of defence in withdrawing the left. The performance or omission of these movements is immaterial; in the works of Gomara, 1845, and Grisier, 1847, it is recommended to offer the opening (as here laid down) from the position of defence.

★★★★★★★★★★

Both rise to the upright position, by bringing the right heel to the left, salute in *quarte* and *tierce*, and towards each other, as before, and fall on guard. He who first attacked now parries, presenting his point, as in reposting, and as before explained. Upon the termination of thrusting, after the second performance of "one, two," both regain the upright position, move the left foot one step backwards, falling on guard; sound two calls with the right foot, bring the left foot up to the right foot, again assuming the upright position, salute in *quarte* and *tierce*, fall on guard, the right foot from the left, repeat the two calls with the foot, bring the left foot to the right, reassuming the upright position, and at the same time salute each other by bringing the hilt, in *quarte*, up to the mouth, turning the hand to *tierce*, and lowering the hilt slowly towards the right hip.

Left-handed fencers should commence their salute in *tierce*, for were they to commence in *quarte* the order of the salute would appear somewhat distorted, owing to the two fencers presenting their swords in the same line together. Under the same circumstance the first *longe, i.e.,* in taking distance, should be performed with the opposition of *tierce*, and with the nails turned down.

Practising the counters of *quarte* and *tierce* is a similar and advantageous exercise. In this performance the fencers may dispense with the salute, should wear their masks, and *longe* alternately upon each other with the intention of touching, but always waiting until the position of defence is *perfectly* recovered before passing the disengagement. After a few thrusts, on both sides, from the engagement of *quarte*, and upon which the counter of *quarte* should be always taken, the players should change their engagement to that of *tierce*, when, upon the disengagement and *longe*, the counter of *tierce* becomes the necessary parry.

This practice may also be varied by first engaging in half-circle or *seconde*, and by performing the counter of those parries upon the disengagements passed over the *forte* of the blade into the opposite low lines.

THE ASSAULT

Or fencing for hits with the foil, somewhat resembles an encounter with the sword, but is not intended exactly to represent the duel. In actual combat mutual hits may, of course, prove equally fatal, or a hit upon any part of the person may terminate the conflict, whereas in the assault hits are only acknowledged in conformity with the rules of fencing. To contract, however, a habit of close parrying, and to acquire a fatal play with the point it is advisable upon most occasions to adhere to the rules of fencing.

In selecting from the number of parries and multiplicity of performances usually taught as exercises with the foil, those movements which are most useful to the fencer, when engaged in the assault, it will be found that the parries of *quarte* and *tierce* with their counters described with the point in oval form, and passed in their course through the low and high lines equally, or upwards and downwards from the hip to the forehead, are sufficient for forming a very good defence (the other parries being only variations of *quarte* and *tierce*), while the disengagements (simple and counter), the change of engagements (single and double), the beat, and the direct thrust comprise almost all that is necessary for the attack. Those, therefore, who may be imperfect in their knowledge of fencing, but desirous of acquiring a readiness in the practice of the assault, may advance themselves in their object by attending to the following suggestions:

To engage out of the immediate reach of the adversary, or by falling on guard in withdrawing the left foot, but always by crossing the foil, if possible, in the engagement of either *quarte* or *tierce*.

To oppose a guard relative in height to that of the antagonist's; for to present a high guard to a low, or a low to a high, or to thrust high when the adversary's point is presented in the low lines, or to thrust low when his point is presented in the high lines, would be sharing dangers which it is the object to avoid.

To force the adversary to an engagement by threatening him with the point should he show a disinclination to cross the blade, and in such case by no means to *longe* without obtaining either a certainty of advantage over him in reach, or in the opposition of the blade, the fencer's only safeguard in a mutual attack.

To attack the adversary's blade with a sharp beat when he has been compelled to raise his point, and to *longe* in the opening thus obtained.

To conduct the attack (the blades being crossed) chiefly by the changes of engagement of *quarte* and *tierce* when the adversary's point is presented in the high lines, or above the hilt, and of *seconde* and half-circle when his point is presented in the low lines, or beneath the hilt.

To advance with caution (usually on the second change) and in accordance with the adversary's retreat.

★★★★★★★★★★

In changing the engagement, as in parrying, the hand is usually turned from supination to pronation, according to the fencer's choice; he need not, however, at first, when practising the assault, trouble himself as to the exact position of the hand, provided he effects the action with one or other of the edges or his foil. The change of engagement should be generally performed with the point or *foible* of the blade, the fencer being prepared at the same time to bring the *forte*, if necessary, into the line of opposition.

★★★★★★★★★★

To observe with respect to "measure," that the shorter fencer may be touched while unable to reach his opponent, and that while the taller fencer has the advantage in the attack, the object of the shorter should be chiefly to parry and return the repost.

To be always ready to parry (if deceived while performing the change) by either continuing the circular action *once* round in the same course, and immediately after changing it into the opposite direction. Or by at once directing the counter-action into the contrary course, avoiding in most cases (and always when within measure), the repetition (or doubling) of the circular or oval parries in the same line. Doubling the counter, especially that of half-circle high, may, however, be occasionally practised, while retiring, or when the adversary rushes in stabbing on his attack, in which case the counter may be advantageously followed with the parry of *seconde*.

The change of engagement being similar in action to the counter-parries, when performed with a sharp, close beat, whether from the position of defence, while on the advance, or on the retreat, impedes the play of the adversary in his attack, and arrests the course of any premeditated parries, or of doubling in his defence. In thus changing the engagement and parrying with the opposite counters, the fencer is certain to meet with his adversary's attack in one or another of the lines of defence, and from that line the repost should be in most cases immediately delivered. (A similar method is adopted in the exercise of sparring, *i.e.,* in throwing off the attack on the right and left, feigning, and putting in the attack whenever an opening is obtained.) The fencer must not, however, in his first endeavours be disconcerted upon finding his foil frequently jarred and crossed in the adverse sense (contraction).

★★★★★★★★★★

The term contraction is frequently applied to a jarring effect product by an abrupt collision of the weapons in the mutual performance of similar actions (usually half-circular), and by which one or both of the opponents may be even disarmed. The term is also applied, and perhaps more correctly, to an irregular manner of parrying with the circles, *i.e.*, by passing the point *over* instead of *under* the adversary's blade, or *vice versâ*, and by which action the weapons are linked, or drawn together. This may be better understood by the following explanations The counter-parries in the high lines (counter-*quarte* or counter-*tierce*) should always be commenced in passing the point *under* the adversary's blade.

Thus upon a disengagement, high, from the engagement of *quarte*, the proper counter-parry is the counter of *quarte*; if we attempt the counter of *tierce*, we parry by contraction. Again, upon a disengagement, high, from *tierce*, the proper counter-parry is the counter of *tierce*; if we attempt the counter of *quarte*, we parry by contraction, or, whenever we meet the adversary's blade with the parry of either *quarte* or *tierce*, and instead of delivering the repost, exert a binding and circling action downwards upon his blade, we parry by contraction; drawing the opponent's point within our own lines of defence, and consequently with danger towards ourselves. Contraction may be purposely employed, but cannot be always avoided.

It is constantly and accidentally occurring, especially in the performance of the semi-counter parries (usually partaking, more or less, of contraction in their effect), for with whatever precision the circular parry may be commenced, any sudden change of action on the part of the adversary may place the weapons in momentary entanglement. Indeed, the least change in the relative positions of the guard or point may cause a contraction of the parry, which otherwise would be correct in its course.

A frequent recommendation of the fencing-master may, however, be here repeated: "Parry as little as possible by contraction;" and it may be added, but do not be disconcerted when the occurrence takes place. It is better to parry by contraction than to fail altogether in the defence; and the fencer should be prepared upon disengaging to meet with (and should practise to avoid) the circular parry, in its regular or irregular course, *i.e.*, either to the right or to the left.

★★★★★★★★★★

To parry well and in the correct lines will demand a practice of some time, but by degrees the eye and hand will acquire sufficient quickness to enable him to avoid or meet the adversary's blade by counter-disengaging and by directing the parry in its proper course, to put into practice the nicer performances of attack, and to execute more skilful combinations of defence, commencing or terminating them with the sharp action of the simple parry. It is difficult to support the defence with the use of the simple parries alone, especially when the blades are separated, and the fencer is deprived of the guidance he might otherwise avail himself of by his sensibility of touch in the junction of the weapons.

Since, therefore, to follow precisely the adversary's point from one line to another with the *blade* is impracticable; the movements of his point should be followed with the eye alone, and the simple parry attempted only on the termination of the attack. It is to avoid the difficulty of following the opponent's feints in all directions, that the circular or oval parries are performed.

With a similar view (to lessen difficulties) the fencer is recommended, when on the attack, to relinquish all idea of passing his point through a multiplicity of parries, to await the termination of their course, and to deliver his thrust at the first pause in his adversary's action. Furthermore:

To avoid the habit of timing; to time as a rule, only, when the adversary rushes in on the attack, or to time him upon his preparation of attack (before the attack is commenced), usually denoted by some preliminary movement. To execute the *remise* only when the adversary steps away from the attack and steps in again to attack in his turn, or is otherwise unusually slow or wide in his return.

To whip along the blade in *tierce*, or wrench over it from the engagement of *quarte* with an action similar to that in the parry of *seconde*—when the adversary engages with a straightened arm, or attempts to arrest the attack by an extension of the sword arm.

To beat sharply, or press with the *forte*, upon the *foible*—when the

THE POSITIONS
of

DEFENCE
& parry.

ATTACK
& lunge

IN QUARTE
WITH THE COUNTER
AND
IN TIERCE WITH THE COUNTER.

object is to obtain a wider opening in the line of the engagement. To beat lightly with the *foible* on the *forte*—when the object is to disengage upon the adversary's counter beat.

To disengage into the opposite line—when the adversary attempts to beat.

To receive the adversary's first change of engagement, and to disengage and *longe* upon his second change—when he conducts his attack by the changes. To slip away the left foot in a pass to the rear, maintaining the sword in a forced opposition by the elevation of the hand, in disengaging upon the adversary when he changes on his advance.

To attack with a direct thrust when the adversary changes the engagement in close measure.

To yield the wrist and blade to the adversary's action without quitting his weapon—when he attacks by encircling the blade, for by yielding the wrist, the sword is brought round again to the original engagement.

To turn the hand from pronation to supination, or *vice versâ*, and to thrust at the same time in an angular direction along the adversary's blade, when he closes with a strong pressure of his *forte* (the only instance in which this manner of thrusting should be attempted); or to pass the pummel, from *quarte*, around his blade and with an elevation of the hand to plunge the point upon him in the thrust of *tierce*.

To precede the repost with a beat or wrench—when the adversary improperly rests upon his *longe*, with the purpose of counter-parrying in that position or of redoubling his attack—for whenever the adversary rests upon a restrained *longe*, more caution than usual is necessary in delivering the return.

To regain the position of defence immediately after the *longe* (whether successful or not in the attack), keeping the hand on a level with the line of the attack, and bringing the point at once in front of the adversary, from which position the outside counter parry or circle (as the quickest and safest defence) may be formed by the slightest movement of the wrist.

To avoid over longeing, throwing forward the head, or turning aside the face, for when once the eye loses the passing action of the weapons, the fencer is for that moment at his opponent's disposition.

To be guided in accordance with the strength of the limbs as to the exact width of guard or distance between the feet; a wide guard placing the fencer firmer in his position of defence, but restricting the quickness of his development in the *longe.*

To be guided according to the proximity of the adversary in the degree of inflexion given to the elbow, the nearer the sword hand is withdrawn to the body, the better the *forte* meets the adversary's *foible,* while on the other side the space of defence is widened; a free action of the elbow joint, with a lively play of the hand in advancing and withdrawing the point, is, however, always advantageous, by threatening and perplexing the opponent.

To pass the point, in feigning, close along the adversary's blade from one side of it to the other; or to feign the semblance of a disengagement by a turn of the wrist in quitting for a momentary absence the adversary's blade, and in so doing to observe his usual manner of parrying, so as to preconceive and execute the attack upon him.

To simulate a manner of parrying so as to induce the adversary to adopt his attack accordingly, and to frustrate that attack by a preconceived parry and repost.

To bear in mind that all disengagements made under the wrist are attended with greater danger (in quitting the opposition), than those made close along the blade. That it is easier to cut over the point when the adversary's guard is placed low and his point high, *i.e.,* when the *forte* is near the opponent's *foible,* and easier to thrust the disengagement past the blade when the point is near his *forte,* and that therefore the fencer should be always observant of these respective positions.

To observe, with regard to the *forte* and *foible* of the blade, that although as a rule (of which the value is confirmed in practice) the parries should be performed with the *forte,* yet that it is dangerous to leave the line of defence and wander after the adversary's *foible.* That by the pressure of the fingers on the grip, the blade should be held securely, and a power exercised over it from point to hilt, and that when such is the case, a very slight advantage with the *forte* over the adversary's *foible* is sufficient either to command the line of defence in opposition, or to effect the parry and the repost.

That the opposition of the blade when the point only is engaged (and the fencers are out of measure), is not of importance, and that, although it should be carefully maintained when once in measure, it should not be exaggerated, because thereby the opening would be unnecessarily widened in the opposite line.

To remember that the opposition is not only formed by the direction given to the blade to the right and to the left, but also by the elevation of the hand; particularly when the thrust is delivered with the hand in pronation.

To understand with respect to left-handed fencers, that with them the lines of defence and parries are only changed in appellation, and that left-handed players can perform, with equal facility, everything that can be done by the right-handed man.

To bear in mind, when opposed to a left-banded man, that the swordsman need not pay much regard to the hand by which the adverse weapon is held, he has but, in the usual manner, to watch the hilt, to find the blade, to turn aside the point, and to deliver the attack in whichever line the opportunity may offer.

Finally, to engage as much as possible with all kinds of fencers, not only with regular but also with irregular players, until accustomed to resist without flinching, the shock of violent attacks; above all to adhere to the practice of the lesson, for it is by the lesson only that the fencer can be formed.

Clothing and Equipment.

The fencer should be attired in easy clothing, but should wear a stout leather jacket to avoid the possibility of accidents occurring from the breakage of his opponent's foil. For the same reason the mask should be of strong wire and of twisted mesh. When opposed to a violent and irregular player, a leather thigh pad is also a necessary protection.

The padded glove should fit well, and the inner part covering the fingers and palm should be of very pliable leather, upon which a small portion of powdered resin may be sprinkled previous to the assault, for the purpose of assisting the fencer in his hold upon the grip.

The shoes should be also of soft leather for the 'uppers,' and of stout buff for the soles. (The sole of the right shoe is frequently made with a padded flap, to protect the toes from inconvenience in the fall of the foot; this addition to the shoe is not, however, of necessity.) Shoes of this description are best adapted for fencing upon boarded flooring, but light shoes of the usual description are quite suitable when fencing is practised, as it should sometimes be, out of doors. Besides these equipments the fencing-master should be provided with a well-padded *plastron*, or leather *cuirass*, upon which the pupil during his lesson directs his foil.

The Manner of Mounting the Foil.
(Or, fixing Pummel, Hilt, Handle, and Blade together.)

135

Every fencer should know something about mounting a sword or foil. Every fencing-master should be able to mount a sword or foil well, A very little practice will enable him to do so. He should first screw the tang of the foil in the vice, with the flat of the blade to his face, and by gentle pressure bend the foil slightly from the straight line, so that the tang may run in some degree with the curve of the handle. He should next place the tang sideways in the vice, with the blade on his left, and by bending the foil a little inwards give it an inclination in *quarte*; the point being thus thrown downwards and to the left, the foil is rendered more convenient to the hand than if mounted perfectly straight.

The guard should be next passed down the tang to the shoulder of the blade, and should the aperture not be sufficiently large it should be increased by the file, as the shoulder of the tang should in no case be weakened by reduction; should the aperture be so large as to leave a looseness between the guard and the tang, a piece of soft stout leather may be passed down the tang to rest upon the guard. The grip or handle should be next driven down with a mallet, and by the aid of a wooden socket, or a spare handle. Should any space then be found in the tang hole of the grip it must be carefully filled up with a few splinters of wood, as the slightest looseness in the handle mars the mounting of the weapon.

The pummel should be next fixed on. The *end* of the tang may without injury be filed if too thick to pass through the aperture in the pummel. When, on the contrary, any space remains between the tang and the pummel, the vacancy must be also filled up with a splinter or two of wood. It then only remains to nip, or file off the projecting portion of the tang to within the eighth of an inch of the pummel, and with a few light taps of the hammer rivet all the parts together. A piece of soft leather tied neatly over the button or blunted end of the blade, or a piece of thick parchment fitted on in a moistened state (*gutta percha* is sometimes employed for the purpose) completes the work and renders the foil fit for use.

The best foil blades are manufactured at Solingen, and those numbered 5 are mostly made use of. (The blade from shoulder to point should not exceed in length 34 inches, at most.) Open guards of iron, slightly bent upwards, or towards the point, for the better protection of the thumb, are generally used in fencing, and are more convenient than close ones. Twisted twine is the best covering for the handles, which are made of different sizes, slightly curved and more or less squared or flattened. The handle should in no case be rounded, nor should it be too much tapered towards the pummel; it should be of nearly uniform size throughout. Lastly, the pummel should not be over large, and only sufficiently weighty to balance the blade when placed on the forefinger, between two and three inches from the guard.

PART 2

PREFATORY OBSERVATIONS.

In adopting a course of instruction by which the art of fencing may be simplified, and at the same time the principles expressed in the foregoing part adhered to, the following performances may be selected. The position when on guard, the *longe*, and recovery to the position of defence; the engagement, change of engagement, direct thrust, disengagement, counter disengagement, and cut over point, with the occasional introduction of a simple feint or beat upon the blade. In the defence:—*tierce*, with its counter (or the outer circle), and *quarte*, with its counter (or the inner circle), should be principally employed. In parrying during the action of recovering from the *longe*, the outer circle is, however, preferable to the inner. All other parries are but variations of *quarte* and *tierce* in lowering and raising the point.

At the same time the pupil should be shown, and he should occasionally practise those variations designated parries, under the terms of *prime*, half-circle, and *seconde*; for although with the circular parries of *quarte* and *tierce*, a perfect defence may be formed in the management of the small-sword or light blade of three edges, it is not always possible to form, with these parries alone, a sufficient defence in the use of the flat and heavier blade of modern warfare.

Fencing is not only an invigorating and intellectual pastime, but also a guide to the management of all weapons of point and edge; it is therefore as well that the plan of defence, especially in military schools, should comprise the parries of *prime, seconde, tierce, quarte*, and half-circle, so that the pupil may obtain as much as possible, while practising with the foil, a general knowledge of the use of the sword.

For this reason, also, the simple parries of *tierce* and *seconde* (for the defence of the outside lines) should be generally performed with the hand in pronation, and the parries of *quarte* and half-circle (for the defence of the inside lines), with the hand more or less in supination, the parry of *prime* for the defence against a high thrust inside, or against a cut delivered at the head, being always effected with the hand in pronation. By these observances the fencer, in parrying with the foil, acquires also the manner of directing the edge in parrying and cutting with the sabre, an advantage difficult to obtain in playing with the stick.

To learn the true position of the edge in the parry, and to accustom the wrist to the use of the actual sword, the lesson should be occasionally practised with light sabres or small-swords, properly mounted and buttoned. By this exercise the pupil will attain that facility in the turn of the wrist so fatal to an adversary when the direction of the edge is changed immediately after the parry, or in the momentary interval which usually follows the collision of weapons. All sword parries (whether of the broad or smallsword) are similar in position, but when practising the fencing lesson with the sword blade, the pupil should be shown that to parry a sabre cut it is necessary to make use of a *beating* action, *so as to meet the antagonist's attack.*

The simple *resistance* of the blade, though sufficient to turn aside a thrust, may be forced down by a violent blow; whereas a light beat, properly timed, will arrest or throw back a heavy cut. It should also be shown, that in cutting with the sabre, the thumb may be occasionally shifted from the arch to the side of the handle, and that the fingers may likewise be, more or less, clasped round the grip in accordance with its size, as well as with regard to the weight of the sword-blade— the turn of the wrist supplying the loss of that action of the fingers which is exercised in the use of a very light weapon.

By thus practising the fencing lesson with the sword-blade, a quickness and strength of hand will also be acquired in delivering, and, what is of great consequence, in recovering the point, which should be as rapidly withdrawn as it is darted forward.

Many of the attacks and parries taught with the foil may be also practised with the bayonet. Indeed, with proper appliances, the use of the bayonet may be demonstrated in a somewhat similar manner to that by which the lesson is given with the foil—the difference in the position of defence, *i.e.,* the left foot in advance, being of course allowed for, and the volt or spring to the right or left occasionally put in practice; for though volting is prohibited in teaching with the foil, and condemned in fencing, because the play of the smallsword is too close and rapid to admit of shifting with safety, yet in the wider motion of cutting with the sabre, and the slower action of thrusting with the bayonet, the volt becomes at times a necessary movement, which may be easily regulated by the master.

These exercises with the sword and with the bayonet should not, however, be introduced into the fencing lesson until the pupil has made some progress in the practice of the foil. The following instructions are sufficient as initiatory lessons, previous to the practice of loose play. They may be enlarged to an almost endless extent, according to the pupil's capability, but it is useless to describe in print, lessons of a more complicated kind. Abstruse definitions in writing, only perplex the pupil, while the fencing-master capable of understanding their meaning, is at the same time himself able to compose and vary the lesson without seeking instructions from the book.

The ensuing exercises, on the contrary, may be easily understood, and are designed for the assistance of inexperienced fencers in the mutual instruction of each other, or for the use of fencing-masters unacquainted with the French language. The lessons and explanations however, although not so long in practice as they appear in print, demand a little application in studying them.

First or Preparatory Lesson.

In this lesson the mask may be dispensed with, but whenever the lesson is practised on the *plastron* it is *advisable that the mask should be worn by both teacher and pupil.*

Position of Defence, the *Longe*, Advance, and Retreat.

The pupil having been shown the manner of holding his foil, and having had the difference between the *forte* and *foible* explained to him, should be placed in the upright or preliminary position, supporting his foil by the hilt in the left hand on the left hip, somewhat after the manner in which the sword is carried in the scabbard. From this position he should be conducted in separate motions (see Part 1) to the position of defence; or when the preparatory lesson, is given in class, the pupils should be formed in single rank with intervals of about two paces, and should assume the position of defence, "on guard," by word of command: thus:—

1. Pass the sword-hand across the body and grasp the grip.

2. Raise both hands above the head, retaining their hold upon the grip and hilt.

3. Bend the elbows and knees.

4. Bring the sword's point to the front, the hilt opposite the breast, the fingernails turned up; withdraw the left arm slightly, and advance the right foot.

In this position the pupil should next.be taught to advance by the right foot, and to retire by the left; afterwards the *longe*, on attack, in four motions:—

1. Straighten the sword-arm, the point lowered, the hilt in a line with the left shoulder.

2. Lower the left arm.

3. Straighten the left knee.

4. Advance the body with the right foot, grazing the floor and sounding the fall; the bust and head erect, the glance directed over the forearm.

Lastly. The recovery from the *longe* to the position on guard.

Recover—

1. Bend the left knee.

2. Bend and raise the left arm.

3. Spring back (without straightening the knees) to the position of defence.

4. Bend the right elbow. These performances (explained more fully in Part 1) should next be executed in two motions, and, when understood, with simultaneous action and the greatest rapidity.

This lesson may be terminated after sufficient repetition by the pupil Or pupils coming to the salute:—

1. Beating twice with the right foot.

2. Springing to the upright position (in bringing the left foot to the right heel), and lowering the left arm.

3. Carrying the hilt to the mouth (the hand in *quarte*).

4. Lowering the foil outside of the right hip (the hand in *tierce*).

Lesson 2

Lines of Defence—Simple Parries—Reposts with and without Longeing—
The Direct Thrust, Disengagement, Beat, and Pressure of the Blade.

The pupils must now be taught separately by word and action, and in directing the foil upon the *plastron*. (The instructor passing his point into the opposite lines, in accordance with his directions to the pupil, and in opposition to the pupil's movement.)

This lesson comprises the simpler movements of fencing, which, as the principles of swordmanship, should be understood before practising the strict play of the foil. In giving the lesson, the instructor should be careful in keeping his foil to the front, or presented towards the pupil, so that the pupil may be, in a manner, compelled to observe the opposition of the blade. While the pupil is practising upon the *plastron*, the instructor should also himself maintain the position of defence, and should vary his action in longeing out, or in merely passing his point towards the pupil, who should be accustomed, by degrees, to its approach. The instructor cannot be too particular throughout, in correcting any irregularity in the pupil's positions of attack and defence.

Placed on guard, the pupil should be shown the manner or engaging (in *quarte*) without pressing unduly upon the weapon opposed to him; the touch of the blade, and the opposition in the engagement, should be explained, and he should be shown how, in a forced engagement (when in measure), the *forte* of the blade is employed, and how, when out of distance, the point only is engaged. He should be then instructed in the knowledge of the lines of defence, and in the performance of the simple parries after the following manner:

Engaged in *quarte* (the inside line high), press my blade lightly—you have the advantage in the engagement or opposition; you are protected, and I am exposed. I therefore *disengage*, by directing my point under your wrist, or with the intention of passing to the opposite side of your blade. Before my point is raised, lower your own without any movement of the shoulder by the action of the wrist and fingers, with the nails up, and in straightening the arm.

You have parried, *half-circle*, in the inside line low, and I am prevented from touching you...... I *disengage* by passing my point over the *forte* of your blade. Turn your nails down, pass the hilt a little to the right, on the same level, and catch my blade with the *forte* of your own; you have parried *seconde* in the outside line low, and I am still unable to touch you...... I therefore disengage by raising my point above your hilt.

Raise your hand and point, bending the elbow, and catching my blade with the *forte* of your own. You have parried *tierce* in the outside line high, and I am again prevented from touching you..... I therefore again disengage by directing my point past your blade. Turn your nails to the left, and on the same level pass your point and hand a little to left, catching my blade with the *forte* of your own. You have parried *quarte* (in the inside line high), the original engagement, and thus closed alternately each line of defence.

The parry of *prime* should be here shown and explained to the pupil as similar to half-circle, (also the variations of these parries, from low to high), but with the nails down instead of up. The instructor may also show how the weapon, placed in any one of the lines of defence, will parry a cut as well as a thrust.

The pupil should next be shown the manner of returning the attack immediately after the parry by the direct repost; but it in not intended that he should be practised in this lesson to execute the repost with rapidity. He will acquire the necessary manner of so doing in subsequent practice.

> Engage in *Quarte.*—Upon my disengagement and *longe,* parry half-circle (slightly lifting my blade), and, without moving head, body, or foot, touch me in the inside line low (beneath my hilt) . . . . . As I recover withdraw your point, still in the engagement of half-circle, feeling my blade lightly . . . . Upon my disengagement and *longe* over your *forte,*—parry *seconde,* turn up the fingernails, raise the hand, close the line of opposition in *tierce,* and touch me in the outside line high (or over my arm). . . . . As I recover, engage in *tierce;* feel my blade lightly. Upon my disengagement to the opposite side of your blade, parry *quarte* by a very slight movement of the hand to the left, the point opposite my right shoulder,—return in the direct line, with the nails up, and with the opposition of *quarte;* upon my recovery, resume the engagement of *quarte,* feeling my blade lightly. . . . Upon my disengagement to the opposite side of your blade, parry *tierce* by a slight movement of the hand to the right; return in the direct line, observe the opposition (the nails either up or down), and resume the engagement in *tierce.*

The parry and repost, or return attack executed with the *longe,* should be next attended to; the instructor regulating the position of the pupil in his *longe,* and not permitting him to lean upon the *plastron,* a moderate bend in the foil being enough to mark the hit. The instructor should on all occasions restrain the pupil from over-longeing; for although the *longe* should be fully developed, all tendency to throw the body forward, or off its balance, should be carefully prevented. The fencer should be able to recover easily from the *longe* to the position of defence; in the performance of which, bending the left knee is almost everything. To obtain length of reach in the attack, and quickness in getting on guard again, the *longe* and *recovery* can hardly be too much practised. In all personal conflict length of reach is undoubtedly of great advantage; but it must be remembered that the equilibrium of the body is of still greater consideration.

From the engagement of *tierce,* upon my disengagement, parry

quarte, wait my recovery, straighten the arm, *longe* in the opposition of *quarte* (touching the *plastron*), the glance directed outside
your arm. Recover in *quarte*, feeling my blade. . . . Upon my
disengagement parry *tierce*, wait my recovery, turn your nails up,
straighten your arm, and *longe* in the opposition of *tierce* (touching the *plastron*), the eye directed inside your arm. Recover in
tierce, feeling my blade. . . . . I press your blade out of line—in
your turn disengage; (by turning the thumb towards your face,
lowering your point, and with the play of the fingers passing
it under my hilt, close to my blade, but without touching it;)
straighten the arm, turn up the nails, keep the opposition, and
longe in *quarte* (touching the *plastron*). Recover in *quarte*. I
press your blade; you must disengage, straighten the arm, turn
up the nails, and *longe* in the opposition of *tierce* (touching the
plastron).

★★★★★★★★★★

A repetition of the direction to touch the *plastron* is unnecessary. The
instructor must be guided by circumstances in giving admittance to
the point or in parrying the attack, obliging the pupil to parry frequently in return or during his recovery to the position of defence.
Quarte and half-circle for the defence of the inner lines, and *tierce* and
seconde for the defence of the outer lines.

★★★★★★★★★★

Recover in *tierce*. . . . I press your blade, at the same time raising
my point; slacken the fourth and little fingers, turn the pummel
slightly towards me, pass the point over my point (cut over),
and *longe* in the opposition of *quarte*. Recover in *quarte*. I
press your blade; cut over my point, and *longe* in the opposition
of *tierce*. . . . . .On guard in *tierce* I press your blade; disengage
without longeing (mark one) as a *feint* only; I attempt to parry
quarte. Do not allow my blade to meet your own, but disengage
again (mark two), and *longe* in the opposition of *tierce*. Recover
in *tierce*. . . . . Repeat the feint (mark one); I attempt to parry
quarte. Do not let me touch your blade, but disengage again
(mark two); I parry *tierce*. You must disengage again without
the blades touching (mark three), and *longe* in the opposition
of *quarte*.

These disengagements should be performed by gradation, and
with a vertical movement of the point advanced according to the
proximity of the adversary's hilt, either around his wrist or immedi-

ately past his blade.

In performing the disengagement as a feint, the arm should be straightened as in the actual thrust, but the disengagement may be itself feinted by a greater or a lesser movement of the point, and the pupil's action in feinting should be thus varied from time to time, the movement proceeding from the actions of hand, wrist, and forearm, and not from the shoulder.

> Engaged in *quarte*, advance one pace as I retire, press lightly on my blade, securing the line of opposition; I yield to your pressure, *longe*, and recover. . . . As I advance, retire in *quarte*, press my blade, if I resist by pressure; you must disengage, *longe*, recover in *tierce*. . . . Beat the *foible* of my blade sharply with the middle of your own; if I yield, *longe* and recover in *tierce*. . . . . Repeat the beat with your *foible* lightly on my *forte*; if I reply,—disengage, *longe*, recover, parrying in *quarte*. . . . Beat lightly, cut over, *longe*, and recover in *tierce*. . . . .Advance one pace, as I retire threaten me with your point without longeing; if I attempt to parry *tierce*,—you must disengage, *longe*, recover in *quarte*. . . . Retire one pace on my advance,—disengage, *longe*, recover in *tierce*. . . . .Advance one pace; as I retire, threaten me with the point.
> Instead of parrying this time, I threaten you in return. Parry yourself, in *tierce*, *longe*, and recover. . . . Retire a pace, disengage, *longe*, and recover.
> Straighten your arm (for the direct thrust), *longe*, and recover. This lesson and also the subsequent lessons should be terminated with a few direct thrusts and disengagements.

It will be observed that although the pupil is taught in this lesson to deceive (marking one, two) his adversary in the performance of the simple parries *tierce* and *quarte*, alternately, he is not instructed to perform himself the defence in that manner, as by so doing a habit might be contracted of wandering with the hand by wide movements from one line to another, whereas when once the pupil has been accustomed to parry with the circle (explained in the following lesson), he will afterwards be able to perform the simple parries with greater precision.

Lesson 3

Counter-parries of *Tierce* and *Quarte*, Counter-disengagements, Changing, and manner of avoiding the change of Engagement,

The pupil having acquired the manner of employing the edge in parrying according to the different descriptions of sword blade, need not in the following lessons develop the turn of the wrist so fully as he has hitherto been called upon to do. He may now, as a general habit in engaging and parrying, maintain a medium position between that of supination and pronation; but although when delivering the repost the hand may occasionally be placed in pronation, the fingernails should be always turned completely upwards in executing the thrust with the *longe* on attack. The instructor having shown the pupil the proper position of the hand, and placed him on guard in *quarte*, will thus proceed.

Engaged in *quarte*, press my blade lightly, close the line; you have the advantage in the engagement, I therefore disengage on attack. Instead of parrying by the simple parry of *tierce* (as in the last lesson), you must parry now with the counter of *quarte*: thus—Retain your position of engagement—with an action of the hand and fingers lower your point, pass it in circular course under my blade, and with a slight beat resume the engagement of *quarte*—without longeing, throw in the repost.

I parry the repost with *quarte*—you must disengage, and *longe* in *tierce*. . . . Recover in *tierce*, press my blade, I disengage. Instead of parrying, as in the last lesson, with the simple parry of *quarte*, you must parry now with the counter of *tierce*, thus— Retain your position of engagement, with an action of the hand and fingers, pass your point in circular course under my blade, and with a light beat resume the engagement of *tierce*; without longeing throw in the repost, I parry the repost with *tierce*, you must disengage, *longe*, and recover in *quarte*. . . . I press your blade, *change the engagement*, thus—Pass your point (as in the action of counter *tierce*) under my blade, and close the line in *tierce*. . . . I press your blade, change the engagement to *quarte* (as in the action of counter-*quarte*), pass your point under my blade, and close the line in *quarte*, ... Double change (change into *tierce*,—change into *quarte*), you command my blade, I am exposed, *longe*.

I parry with *quarte* and I present my point as you recover, parry in changing the line to *tierce* . . . . On guard, I disengage; parry my disengagement with the counter of *tierce* and *longe*; I parry with *tierce*, and as you recover I present my point. Parry me by changing to *quarte*; on guard. ,. . . . parry, counter-*quarte*, *longe*, recover, parry, changing to *tierce*. . . . . On guard, parry, counter-*tierce*, *longe*, recover, parry in changing to *quarte*.

This lesson of parrying with the counter, *longeing*, and again parrying with the counter in *changing the line during the recovery* to the position of defence, should be often repeated. It is an excellent exercise for relaxing the muscles of the forearm, and accustoming the hand to retain its position in parrying by the counters.

★★★★★★★★★★

Changing the line while on the recovery is frequently of advantage in fencing the assault. The change of engagement, however, should not be *invariably* attempted while recovering from the *longe*, and never unless sufficient space or proper measure be preserved between the fencers.

★★★★★★★★★★

Again engaged in *quarte*, Change the engagement to *tierce*—I deceive you by changing also—follow my blade round with your own, resume, and close the line in *tierce*. . . .Change the engagement to *quarte*, I deceive you—follow my blade, resume, and close the line in *quarte*, *longe*, and recover. . . . In your turn, deceive me when I parry by the counters. . . . Engage in *quarte*, straighten your arm, and, without longeing, disengage; I parry with counter-*quarte*—you must counter-disengage—passing your point with a circular advance around my blade and resuming the position of the first disengagement, *longe*; recover in *tierce*. . . . Disengage, straighten your arm, but without longeing. I parry counter-*tierce*—you must counter-disengage with the circular advance, avoid my blade, and *longe* in *quarte*; recover in *quarte*. The same, to deceive me in my parry of counter-*quarte* (or of counter-*tierce*), but this time abbreviate the course of your counter-disengagement by thrusting under my arm; recover. I change the engagement from *quarte* to *tierce*—deceive me in, my intention; change yourself, and close the line, again in *quarte*. I change again—you must disengage, *longe* in *quarte*, recover. Change into *tierce*, disengage, *longe*, recover; change into *quarte*, disengage, *longe*, recover, change into *quarte*, salute.

LESSON 4

Combinations of the Parries and Attacks.

★★★★★★★★★★

Whenever the direction to "disengage" (without longeing) is met with in the following lessons it must be understood as a feint, only, to induce the adversary to follow the movement, so that according to his parry (simple or counter) the actual disengagement of attack (simple or counter) may be immediately executed. But when the manner of counter-disengaging is once understood, the pupil must be practised to perform the counter-disengagement very rapidly, and without pausing between the first and second motion of the point in passing it under the adversary's blade. The term "to double" is sometimes used in lieu of "to *counter*-disengage," and is also applied to the *repetition* of the counter-parries and counter-disengagements in the same line.

★★★★★★★★★★

The pupil will now learn to parry with the circles in continuous action on the right and on the left, returning the repost from the line in which he may meet his adversary's blade. Also, to deceive his adversary in the combinations of simple and counter-parries. The instructor should explain to the pupil that the circular or, more properly, oval parries, are really combinations of simple ones; the circle or oval to the left comprising *quarte* and *seconde*, that to the right *tierce* and half-circle. In performing these parries the lines should be narrowed, by avoiding too close a measure, and maintaining the hilt as much as possible opposite the centre of the right breast, consistently with safety in securing the lines of defence.

> Engage in *quarte*, I disengage—you must parry by the *counter* of *quarte*, I *counter*-disengage, and, therefore, you do not meet my blade. Circle your point immediately to the right (as in the counter of *tierce*), you will meet my blade in half-circle; straighten your arm, *longe*, and recover your point before you. (It is frequently advantageous to advance the hand slightly in the performance of the second circle.)
>
> Again, engaged in *quarte*, repeat the same (the inside circle first and then the outside circle).
>
> This time you miss my blade in half-circle (I avoid it by again disengaging), continue your circle, you catch my blade in *tierce*; you have formed the two circles in continuous action, *longe*, recover in *tierce*.
>
> Engaged in *tierce*, I disengage, you must parry the counter of *tierce*; I counter-disengage, and you do not meet my blade; circle immediately to the left (as in counter-*quarte*), you will meet my blade in *seconde*, turn up the nails, *longe*, and recover.

Again, engaged in *tierce*, repeat the same (the outer and the inner circle); this time you miss my blade in *seconde* (I avoid it by disengaging); continue your circle, you catch my blade in *quarte*, *longe*, and recover.

Or—Engaged in *quarte*,—Change into *tierce*; I disengage. Upon my disengagement, reverse the circle; you catch me in *seconde*, *longe*, and recover.

Or—Engaged in *tierce*, change in *quarte*; I disengage. Upon my disengagement reverse the circle; you catch me in half-circle, *longe*, and recover. In this manner of parrying the action of abrupt contraction is brought into play. (See Part 1.)

In your turn on attack deceive me in my counter-*quarte* (and simple *tierce*.

Engaged in *quarte*, disengage, I parry with the counter of *quarte*, you must counter-disengage; I parry *tierce*, you must disengage again under my wrist, and *longe* in *quarte*, recover in *quarte*.

Deceive me in my *tierce* and counter-*tierce*. engaged in *quarte*, disengage, I parry *tierce*, you must disengage again; I parry the counter of *tierce*, you must counter-disengage, *longe*, and recover, changing into *tierce*.

Deceive me in my counter-*tierce* and *quarte*.

Engaged in *tierce*, disengage, counter-disengage, disengage again, *longe* and recover.

Deceive me in my *quarte* and counter-*quarte*.

Engaged in *tierce*, mark, one, two, counter-disengage, *longe*, and recover.

Deceive me in my consecutive counters of *quarte* and *tierce*.

Engaged in *quarte*, disengage, I parry with the counter of *quarte*, you must counter-disengage to the outside. I reverse the circle to the counter of *tierce*, you must counter-disengage to the inside, *longe* and recover.

From the engagement of *tierce*, disengage, I parry with the counter of *tierce*, you must counter-disengage to the inside, I reverse the circle to the counter of *quarte*, you must counter-disengage to the outside, *longe*, and recover.

In my turn on the attack. Engaged in *quarte*—upon my disengagement parry, with the counter of *quarte*, change into *tierce*, *longe*, and recover in *tierce*. Upon my disengagement, parry with the counter of *tierce*, change into *quarte*, *longe*, and recover in *quarte*. Upon my disengagement, parry with the counter of *quarte*, change into *tierce*, disengage, *longe* in *quarte*, change into *tierce* as you recover—Disengage, *longe* in *quarte*, recover, disengage into *tierce*, *longe*, and recover—*Salute*.

This practice should be frequently repeated; it contains the substance of fencing, *viz*. Parrying with the circle, changing, returning by the repost, or attacking with the *longe*, and again parrying by the change while recovering to the position of defence.

★★★★★★★★★★

Some teachers prefer the simple parry as a quicker means of defence, to the change on recovering. This is, however, a question of distance, for when proper measure is kept in longeing, there is usually time and space (in bringing the hilt at once to the front) to effect the change or circle while recovering; when the change cannot be effected in time to parry a direct repost, the simple parry always comes naturally to the fencer's hand.

★★★★★★★★★★

Pupils thus far advanced may be occasionally formed in single rank and put through the performance of the simple and counter-parries, returning the attack with smartness, longeing, recovering, advancing, and retiring. They may then, in opposite ranks (wearing the mask) practise, at first by word of command, the disengagements and counter parries of *tierce* and *quarte* alternately (see Part 1), and afterwards continue the same, taking their own time.

SUMMARY OF THE FOREGOING LESSONS, OR A SERIES OF MOVEMENTS OF ATTACK & DEFENCE, TO BE PRACTISED SEPARATELY OR BY SELECTIONS, IN LESSONS OF SHORT DURATION.

Of the Attack Principally.

On Guard, engage in *quarte*; to deceive me in my parry of *tierce*; mark one, two, *longe*, recover in *quarte*.

Engaged in *Quarte*.—To deceive me in my *tierce* and counter-*tierce*; mark one, two, counter-disengage, *longe*, and recover in *quarte*.

Deceive me in my counter-*quarte* and half-circle. disengage, counter-disengage, repass over the *forte* of my blade, and *longe* under my hilt with the outside opposition. Recover in *tierce*.

The same.—If I return to *quarte* after my half-circle, cut over, *longe*, and recover.

Engaged in *Tierce*.—Deceive me in my *quarte* and counter-*quarte*; mark one, two; counter-disengage, *longe*, and recover in *tierce*.

Deceive me in my counter-*tierce* and *seconde*; disengage. counter-

149

disengage, under my arm; disengage over (on the outside), *longe*, and recover in *tierce*.

Deceive me with a turn round my blade.—Disengage, cut over, disengage under(in continuous action), *longe*, and recover in *quarte*.

The same from the engagement of *quarte*.—Disengage, cut over, disengage under (in continuous action), *longe*, and recover in *tierce*.

Engaged in *Tierce*.—Beat, disengage (or cut over), *longe* and recover in *quarte*, feign in half-circle (high), beat in *quarte*, *longe* and recover.

Engaged in *quarte*, beat, disengage, *longe*, in recovering, parry half-circle, *longe*, and recover in *quarte*.

Engaged in *Quarte*. Mark one, two, cut over, *longe*, and recover in *tierce*.

Engaged in *Tierce*. Mark one, two, cut over, *longe* under my hilt, recover in *quarte*.

Engaged in *Quarte*. Disengage; I attempt to parry with the counter of *quarte*. Deceive me by counter-disengaging, and *longe*. I parry with *tierce* and return my point in *seconde*. Parry with half-circle in recovering, *longe*, and recover in *quarte*.

Engaged in *Tierce*. Disengage.—I attempt to parry with the counter of *tierce*. Deceive me by counter-disengaging and *longe*. I parry with *quarte*, and return my point in *quarte*. Parry *quarte* in recovering, *longe*, and recover.

Change into *Tierce*. If I deceive you—parry with the counter and *longe*; in recovering parry with half-circle, beat, *longe*, and recover in *quarte*.

Double change, advance with the second change. (The pupil should be frequently practised in this manner, to arrest the time thrust, by parrying while on the advance.) If I deceive you—parry with the counter and *longe*; in recovering envelope my blade with the outer circle; *longe* and recover in *tierce*.

Feint under my hilt in *seconde*, disengage over my arm in *tierce*, *longe* and recover, catch my blade with half-circle, beat in *quarte*, *longe* and recover.

★★★★★★★★★★

The beat in *quarte* may be effected from half-circle by the semi-circular movement of the point upwards, or by clearing the point from under the adversary's blade, with an inward turn of the wrist (as from *prime*), when the repost may be preceded by a beat, or delivered in continuous movement with the parry, as in the action of cutting over.

★★★★★★★★★★

Change into *tierce*, feint *seconde*, disengage over my hilt into *tierce*, disengage into *quarte*, *longe*; in recovering envelope my blade with the outer circle, *longe* and recover.

Change from *quatre* to *tierce*. If I advance with my point or hand high, stop me; *longe* under my hilt or along my blade, and recover in *tierce*.

Retire in *Tierce*. If I change on my advance—change also (stop me), with the *longe* and recover.

Engage in *Quarte*. I feint to disengage—parry counter-*quarte*. If I counter-disengage—(Time me)—Take the opposition, *longe*, and recover in *tierce*.

Engage in *Tierce*. I feint to disengage—parry counter-*tierce*, If I counter-disengage—(Time me)—Slower your point under my hilt, keep the opposition, *longe*, and recover in *tierce*.

Change into *quarte* and longe. If I parry and raise my point to return, repeat your thrust (*remise*) before recovering, touch me and recover in *quarte*; or:

Engaged in *quarte*, disengage *longe*, slide your blade along mine with a lifting action. If I press upon your blade, turn your hand in pronation, and deliver your thrust in *seconde* before recovering. Recover in *tierce*. (The fencer may sometimes assist himself in the performance of the *remise* by feigning to recover in withdrawing the body by a spring of the knees, termed "the retreat of the body.")

If I straighten my arm in the engagement of *quarte*, threatening you with my point, cross over my *foible* with your *forte*, wrench me in *seconde*, turn up your nails, *longe*, and recover in *tierce*, or continue the action in *seconde*, binding my blade in *flanconnade*, *longe*, and recover; or, from the engagement in *tierce*, cross your *forte* over my *foible*, bind my blade in half-circle, *longe* over my arm, and recover.—The instructor should carefully observe that the pupil's hand is well sustained in the delivery of all thrusts on attack.

Of the Defence Principally.

Engaged in *Quarte*. Advance one pace (or near enough to touch me without longeing) upon my disengagement, parry *tierce*, return with the direct thrust. Upon my parrying *tierce* and returning also the direct repost, parry *tierce* again, return, and touch me in the low line under my arm.

In this manner the following exercises (for the purpose of acquiring rapidity in returning the repost) may be practised, the teacher parrying and returning in the proper lines during his instruction.

Engaged in *Tierce*. Upon my disengagement, parry *quarte*, return direct—parry *quarte*, return, touching me under my arm.

Engaged in *Quarte*. Upon my disengagement, parry *tierce*, return direct—parry the outer circle, repost over my arm.

Engaged in *Tierce*. Upon my disengagement, parry *quarte*, return direct, parry half-circle (high), beat, return direct.

Engaged in *Quarte*. Retire one pace (into proper measure). Upon my disengagement, parry with counter-*quarte*, disengage, *longe*. (Upon my parrying with counter-*quarte*, disengaging and *longeing* also in return.) Recover, parry counter-*quarte* again, cut over, *longe*, and recover in *tierce*.

Engaged in *Tierce*. Upon my disengaging—parry counter-*tierce*, disengage *longe*. (Upon my parrying counter-*tierce*, disengaging, and *longeing* in return.) Parry counter-*tierce* again, recover, cut over, *longe*, and recover in *quarte*.

Parry Counter-*Quarte*. I lower my point—parry half-circle low—I raise my point, parry *quarte* again (to preserve the defence on the inside lines.)

The same in continuous action.

Parry Counter-*Quarte*, half-circle, *quarte*, *longe* and recover.

Engaged in *Quarte*. Parry counter-*quarte*, half-circle—I deceive you—retire one pace, parrying the counter of half-circle (the outside circle), beat, *longe*, and recover in *quarte*.

The same—continue the circle and *longe*, or return, over my arm.

The same—continue the circle and return under my arm.

Engaged in *Tierce*, upon my disengagement—parry counter-*tierce*. I lower my point—parry *seconde*; I raise my point—parry *tierce* (to preserve the defence on the outside lines).

The same in continuous action, *longe* and recover.

Engaged in *Tierce*, upon my disengagement parry *quarte*, counter-*quarte*, *tierce*, counter-*tierce*, or *vice versâ*.

The same in continuous action (the opposite counters), return, *longe*, and recover.

★★★★★★★★★★

So called because the outside circle is performed from the inside engagement of *quarte*, and the inside circle, likewise, from the outside engagement of *tierce*. When, however, it is desirable to avoid binding the blade, or parrying by contraction, the opposite counter should be regulated by waiting for a second disengagement in the movement of attack, so that the parry may be effected at the *completion* of the circle.

****

Engaged in *Quarte*, upon my disengagement parry with the flying counter of *quarte*, passing your point in the action of the parry over my point, or towards your left shoulder, return under my arm, *longe* and recover.

Engaged in *Tierce*, upon my disengagement—parry the flying counter, passing your point towards your right shoulder, over my point; return under my arm, *longe* and recover.

Engaged in *Tierce*, if I glide along your blade to enter by force— parry *prime*, yield your wrist and blade, maintain the pressure, circle your point upwards past your left shoulder, beat in *quarte*, return, *longe* and recover.

Engaged in *Tierce*, upon my disengagement—parry counter-*tierce*; upon my counter-disengagement—parry *prime*, beat, *longe* and recover.

Engaged in *Quarte*, your point low. If I bind your blade by crossing over it in *seconde*, and thrusting in *flanconnade*, yield your wrist to my effort, maintain the pressure on my blade; your own will be brought round to *quarte* again, beat, *longe*, and recover.

Engaged in *Tierce*, your point low. If I bind your blade in half-circle thrusting over your arm, maintain the pressure on my blade, turn your hand into *prime*, return under my arm, *longe*, and recover.

Engaged in *Quarte*. Parry twice (double) with the counter of *quarte*, return the repost, change into *tierce*—parry twice with the counter of *tierce*, return the repost—change into *quarte*.

The position of the body, head, and limbs should be carefully attended to throughout all these lessons, rapidity in the execution of which should be increased in accordance with the pupil's progress, and in delivering the repost the line of opposition should be maintained as strictly as circumstances will permit.

THE ASSAULT, AND CONCLUDING REMARKS.

As soon as the pupil is able to perform with tolerable facility those movements which have been described as the chief performances in fencing, he may commence the practice of loose play. In his first assaults he should, however, practise with the master only.

Having been thus separately prepared, the pupils may engage with one another. They will find that with the beat, change, disengagement, *tierce*, *quarte*, and the circle, the assault may be very well sustained. Beginners in fencing the assault must not, however, be discouraged upon finding a difficulty in putting the lesson into practice. The assault is itself a course of study in which the skill is acquired of putting into use the lesson of fencing taught upon the *plastron*.

The usual errors with inexperienced fencers are, closing upon each other, over-longeing, resting upon the *longe*, repeating the attack without regarding the opponent's repost, and withdrawing the arm to deliver the thrust. These irregularities should be strictly prohibited by the instructor. It should be enforced upon the pupil's attention that the swordsman's object is "to hit, and not to be hit," and it should be shown that by resting on the *longe* the sword-arm may be surrendered to the grasp of the opponent's left hand. By adhering to the rules of fencing regular habits are formed, in keeping due measure and in maintaining the point constantly in front of the adversary.

With these observances very little opportunity is afforded, "sword in hand," for irregular play. When accustomed to loose play the pupils may, however, occasionally practise hitting upon any part of the person, and indeed, upon all occasions hits between the neck and hip may be accounted good. The salute may also be abbreviated, by omitting the passes to the rear, the fencers merely saluting, longeing, and parrying, in *quarte* and *tierce*. The assault when properly conducted consists in A attacking and recovering, B parrying and returning the repost, A parrying the repost, and the renewal of attack.

All harsh actions of the hand should be in most cases avoided; wrenching and binding the blade, although sometimes useful performances, should not be constantly practised. A fencer with a light hand, and by a proper application of his weapon, will always tire out a heavy-handed opponent, while sensibility of *touch* in feeling the blade, by which the adversary's intention is often discovered, is an important acquisition There are other qualities essential to the fencer—a *quick eye*, not so much in clearness of vision as in judging distance; *rapidity*, not precipitancy of action; *precision* in terminating the attack without faltering, and above all, *judgment* in penetrating the adversary's designs and in regulating the actions of attack and defence. The possession of *this* advantage rests wholly with the fencer himself; dexterity may be imparted by the teacher, and the eye may be quickened by practice, but judgment can only be obtained through reflection and self-command.

Notes and Observations on the Art of Fencing

By George Chapman

INTRODUCTION

A taste for practising the Art of Fencing has introduction. been for some years slowly, but steadily, increasing. Endeavours have recently been even made to introduce the use of the Foil as one of our military exercises, and many of our volunteer regiments have established Schools of Arms at their headquarters. Proficients in fencing may, therefore, at the present moment, reasonably offer the fruits of their experience towards the furtherance of the art. In so doing; and in continuance of former endeavours, the author of the following observations proposes to explain the principles of fencing, according to the theories of eminent masters, and to expose the errors which have been promoted, or are tolerated by incompetent instructors;—so that the novice may be cautioned against common faults which, when contracted in the early lessons of fencing, are ever after difficult of correction.

In the practice of all bodily exercises a correct application of the physical powers should be the primary consideration, and in the adoption of postures, necessary towards the accomplishments of every physical art, those actions which are the most graceful or pleasing to the eye may be generally taken as the best rules by which to be guided. Now, graceful and just positions of the human frame are in no exercise whatsoever of more consequence than in that of fencing, for upon them chiefly, the success of the fencer depends.

The present number is devoted to the consideration of the positions of attack and defence. A few remarks upon the formation of the small-sword, and its substitute the foil, with an explanation of the manner of grasping the handle, are almost necessarily preliminary to subsequent observation.

All sword-play may be properly designated as Fencing, but the term is usually applied to the management of the small-sword, and to the use of the point in thrusting only.

The small-sword is constructed with three blunt edges upon which the parries are effected, and is hollowed between each edge for the purpose of rendering the blade stiff and light at the same time. By persons who have not given much attention to the construction of sword-blades, or who have not studied the subject of swordsmanship and its progress from past to present times, the small-sword is often confounded with the rapier; and, the weapons. indeed, in modern English dictionaries the word denotes a sword for thrusting with only.

★★★★★★★★★★

In the vocabularies of other countries, the distinction is frequently observed. The German *schläger*, or cutting blade, for instance, is termed a rapier. The small-sword, and modern fencing foil, were introduced during the last century, before which the lesson in fencing was practised with the "Tuck," a rapier blade, narrowed, somewhat increased in solidity, and when blunted designated as a "Foile."

★★★★★★★★★★

This disregard of distinction is unimportant to most people, but, as the Art of Fencing may be considered a foundation for swordsmanship generally, all fencers should understand the relative difference between the rapier and small-sword. For while the small-sword is of triangular formation, and shaped only for thrusting, the rapier, properly speaking, is a flat blade intended for both thrusting and cutting. In the course of instruction, the fencing-master should make it his duty to explain the difference between the triangular and double-edged weapons, so that his pupils may readily apply their abilities in fencing to the management of either kind of blade, as it may casually come to hand.

When the parries with their varied application come to be treated of, the advantage to the fencer in carefully distinguishing the difference alluded to, will be fully explained. Among the various actions which may be conveniently executed with the triangular or duelling sword there are many which cannot be so easily managed with a flat blade, or with the usual weapon of modern warfare, however light in weight that weapon may happen to be. Fencers among military men should be therefore cautioned against *indiscriminately* attempting with the sword the performances usually taught in lessons with the foil.

The foil is a truly quadrangular blade, so formed that, from its pliancy, it may be better adapted for practice than the actual sword. It should measure thirty-four inches from point to hilt. A shorter blade should not be used in practising the lesson. The best form of shell or guard is the ordinary double-ringed open iron one, but both sides of it should be bent upwards to protect the thumb and fingers from injury.—(Careless teachers frequently neglect this precaution.)—The grip or handle should be in length at least seven inches, (including the pummel), almost square, slightly curved, and of nearly uniform size throughout; the convex and concave sides, in a trifling degree, wider than those on the right and left. It should be always (as it usually is), covered with twisted twine of two sizes, and should measure around from 2 to 3 inches according to choice, or the size of the player's hand. The pummel should weigh about 3ozs. and should be barrel-shaped or oblong, rather than globular.

★★★★★★★★★

It has not been thought necessary to explain in these pages the manner of mounting the foil, or fixing the pummel, handle, and guard to the blade. A full description thereof may be found in *Foil Practice*, and recommended to the consideration of the army, by General the Honourable Sir James Yorke Scarlett, Adjutant-General of the Forces, with the sanction of H.B.H. the Field Marshal Commanding-in-Chief.

★★★★★★★★★

The grasp with the fingers, or hold on the grip, should be firm but not strained, the thumb should be laid along the upper or convex side in a line with the point and almost touching the shell. The fingers should be closely pressed against each other upon the left side of the handle. The index should not be separated from the middle finger. A space or hollow should be left in the palm of the hand, between the little finger and the grip. The fingers should not be bent over the upper side of the grip; because, in so doing the play of the foil cannot be managed as it should be by an action of the fingers (principally the thumb, index, and middle finger), but must proceed, as it should not, from the shoulder.

A correct manipulation of the handle of the foil is a difficult attainment, in which even many strong fencers never succeed. Far greater delicacy of grasp is necessary in the use of the small-sword than in the use of a flat blade, or of a heavier weapon. But this is a subject to which indifferent teachers seldom pay attention: indeed, they seldom understand it.

Of the positions in fencing, strictly speaking, there are but two.

That of the defence and that of the attack. As a preliminary position, previous to falling into the position of defence, or, as it is termed, "On Guard," the fencer should place himself in an upright position, the right heel in the hollow of the left ankle, the feet at right angles, the head turned sideways towards the adversary, and the left side of the breast slightly brought round to the front. The shoulders drooping, the arms lowered at the sides, the hilt held in front, and over the right knee.

Bending the knees until the left be on a line with and directly over the toes, the right foot should be advanced (the heel on a line from the left ankle) to a distance of at least twice the length of the fencer's foot, or, for a man of middle height, about twenty inches, so that the right knee may not overhang the instep. The stride should never be less, and when the fencer is not vigorous of frame even more.

In the position of defence, the utmost steadiness must be preserved, to insure which the left hip should be pressed inwards, and the frame supported in a perfectly upright line equally on both legs; attention should also be paid to the position of the right knee, so that it should not bend inwards. As the right foot is advanced the arms should at the same time be raised, the elbows slightly bent, (the left forearm rather more than the right,) the palm of the left hand turned towards the left cheek, the point of the foil presented directly at the adversary's face; the pummel on a line with and opposite the right nipple. From this position the foil may be inclined either to the right or left, according to the line chosen for attack or defence.

★★★★★★★★★★

Similar instructions, with a slight variation in the wording, may be seen in *Foil Practice, viz.*, from the preliminary and upright position. 1. Pass the sword hand across the body and grasp the hilt. 2. Raise both hands above the head, retaining their hold upon the grip and hilt. 3. Bend the elbows and knees. 4. Bring the sword's point to the front, withdrawing the left arm, and advancing the right foot.

★★★★★★★★★★

In these movements, to be lifted. which should be combined, as it were, into one, care should be taken not to lift the shoulders, for the awkward effect of lifting the shoulders deprives a fencer of all lightness of action in attack, and renders his movements forced and clumsy in defence. This ugly fault is also one of the many which careless teachers seldom notice.

Design No. 1 illustrates the position in which the fencer should place himself when 'On Guard,' when parrying, when advancing, and when retiring, nor, as a rule, should the head or body be swerved backwards, forwards, on the right or left, but should be retained in an erect position; so that the eye, though principally fixed upon the adversary's hilt, may not lose sight of his general actions.

Thus placed the fencer may easily and gracefully effect the advance, by first moving the right foot forward and then bringing up the left; or the retreat, by the first moving the left backwards and then withdrawing the right.

In advancing or retreating the knees should be kept bent, and the shoulders carried on a perfect level.

Necessary as it is to support the body in an erect position while 'On Guard,' and whether advancing or retreating, it is of far greater consequence to retain that position, when upon the attack in the performance of the longe. To effect that performance—

First: The sword-arm should be straightened without straining it, and without lifting the shoulders, the pummel on a level with the shoulder, the fingernails turned upwards, the hand borne either on the right or left according to the line of attack, the point directed at the opponent's breast. Secondly: The left shoulder and arm should be lowered, the hand open, the knuckles inclined towards the left knee. Thirdly: The left knee should be completely straightened. Fourthly: The right foot advanced two lengths of the fencer's foot, or four times the length of the foot from heel to heel—(with a man of middle height at least forty inches in the stride)—the right knee remaining fixed and perpendicular to the instep.

These movements, when understood, should be combined with the greatest possible rapidity, the head and body supported in an erect position throughout; the bust slightly turned towards the opponent and the left foot retained, toe and heel, to the ground (*vide* Design, No. 1); care should be taken that the left foot be neither raised, dragged forward, nor slipped backwards, and that the sword-arm be advanced previous to the right foot.

The support of the head and bust in longeing is, perhaps, one of the most difficult attainments in fencing. Most fencers—even the most skilful, are apt, in the eagerness of attack, or from momentary loss of nerve, to throw themselves forward, but this dangerous habit cannot be too sharply denounced, or too carefully guarded against.

★★★★★★★★★★

Some foil players, under the protection of the mask, adopt this move-

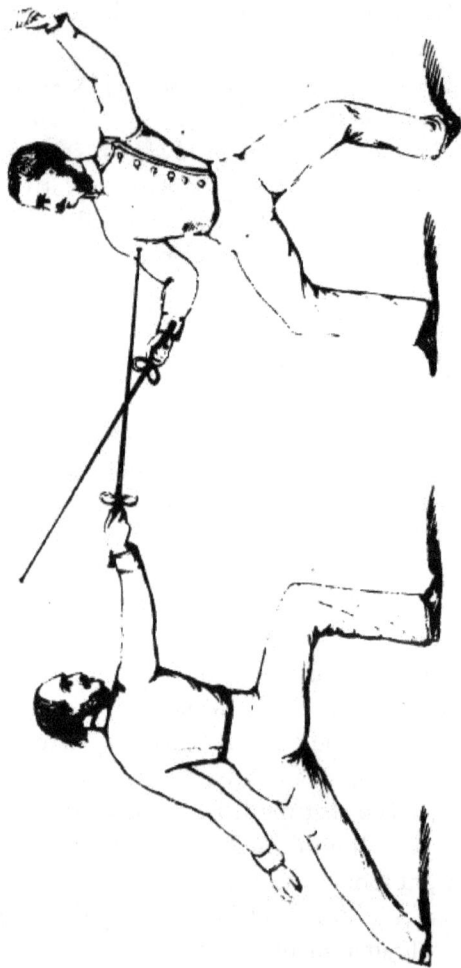

Design Nº 1.

Positions.

Of attack with the Lunge.   and   of Defence with a Parry in Carte.

Design Nº 2.

Design Nº 3.

Danger incurred in throwing the head and shoulders forward on the Lunge.

ment as a practice, purposely to cover the breast, and in abuse of the conventional rules of fencing, by which hits are only allowed when delivered on the bust. In such cases all hits upon any part of the person, above the hips, should be accounted good. In parrying, three-quarters of the bust should be presented towards the adversary—in the attack somewhat less. The attack should not be avoided by shifting one part of the body to the exposure of another, but by parrying the opponent's thrust.

★★★★★★★★★★

1st, it is most ungraceful in appearance. 2nd, it throws the fencer off his balance. 3rd, it surrenders his sword arm to his antagonist's grasp, see Design, No. 2. 4th, it exposes his head to the opponent's point, see Design No. 3. 5th, it prevents the fencer from recovering with ease or safety to the position of defence. 6th, it deranges his sword-arm, so that while recovering he cannot parry the antagonist's return attack. 7th, it precludes the opposition of the blade. 8th, it confuses the mind; for in lowering the head, the passing action of the contest is to a great extent lost to the eye.

Lastly, if the bust be lowered in longeing, it must be raised in recovering, a double action attended with great risk, and certain to retard the fencer's retreat after having recovered, or his advance after having longed.

To recover to the position of defence, the frame should not be *tossed upwards* or lifted by the shoulders, but *drawn backwards*—through bending the left knee—a muscular exertion of the left thigh, and by lifting the right foot with a slight pressure from the ground. Thus, the fencer retains a level carriage both in the attack and defence. At the same time that the right foot is replaced on the spot it originally occupied, the sword-arm should be again slightly bent, and the left arm raised and placed as before, acting somewhat as a balance, *i.e.*, rising during the recovery, and falling with the longe.

In advocating a strict observance of the proper grasp, or manipulation of the foil handle, and also of the maintenance of the head and body in an erect position, it must, however, be allowed that finished Fencers occasionally permit themselves a certain licence in relaxing or slightly changing the hold upon the grip. In feigning or parrying, they also occasionally advance or withdraw the bust. For the guard may be partly offensive or wholly defensive. It is termed offensive when the point is directly presented at the adversary, in which action the bust is sometimes slightly advanced: Defensive, when the point is raised with the sole intent on the part of the fencer to parry, and in which action the head is often slightly thrown back.

Duellists also occasionally adopt the trick of dropping the head or stretching the body forward, preferring the greater chance but lesser injury of being wounded on the shoulder to the less chance but more serious consequences of being hit below the waist. But it must be remembered that the duel is usually conducted on ground selected for the purpose, and with seconds at hand to enforce the observance of conventional rules, by which, not only is the combat generally terminated at the first wound, however slight, but, all use of the left hand in grasping the adversary, or any attempt to wound an opponent who may have stumbled or fallen, is forbidden.

The case is different, however, on slippery or rough ground or when no friend is near to interpose, and it may be easily conceived that a bold and erect carriage must be to a soldier in action, whether mounted or on foot, of primary importance—so that he may keep his eyes about him and not throw himself out of his saddle or off his balance. Further, it may be remarked that a sword thrust should not be delivered with a deadweight-like or slouching push, such as must be the case when the head and shoulders are thrown forward, but darted from the shoulder with a sharp light stroke, so that the weapon may be easily extricated and brought to a position in which, if necessary, a parry may be readily effected.

★★★★★★★★★★

That a man may be desperately wounded and yet retaliate upon his enemy has been frequently witnessed in action.

In the historical record of a duel which took place in 1613, between Lord Bruce and Sir Edward Sackville, it is related, that before Lord Bruce was in the slightest degree hurt, Sir Edward Sackville had received no less than three severe wounds, and yet overcame his adversary. Lord Bruce was slain through his inability to withdraw his sword which had, in Sir Edward Sackville's own words, "entered my right pap and passed through my body."

★★★★★★★★★★

The irregularities, therefore, which, as before stated, practised fencers occasionally commit, must be regarded as exceptions—not as rules—and although an infringement of rule must be expected, and even to some extent tolerated in loose play, no irregularities should be permitted in the lesson. Above all, a neglect on the part of an instructor, in permitting a pupil to abandon his position while on the longe, is most reprehensible. This negligence is never permitted by skilful fencing masters, but is often overlooked by indifferent teachers, either from carelessness or through not understanding the true principles of fencing; for the mere fact of *professing* to teach does not constitute a man a fencing master in the true acceptation of the term.

To justly assume that title a man should have served for some years as an assistant under a professor of repute, or at least have gained a reputation for himself in frequent and public trials of his merits before competent judges. Even then excellence in fencing may not prove capability in teaching. Yet, certainly, no man should claim to be a good instructor who cannot prove himself a first-rate fencer.

When an instructor has neither had the advantage of acquiring experience as an assistant, nor the opportunity of gaining it through long practice with fencers and masters of public note, he naturally overlooks the nice but necessary points of fencing.

A loss of activity will, of course, result from age or infirmity. But, to command the respect due to eminence in their art, fencing masters advanced in years, should have been at least remarkable in earlier life among the principal swordsmen of their day.

Certificates of capability are not to be trusted, and, indeed, they may be regarded, unless signed by conscientious and eminent masters, as worse than worthless. Men are to be met with who can exhibit Certificates of Proficiency as masters, and yet cannot place themselves properly on guard—pass a disengagement with exactness—or reason in the slightest degree on the theory of fencing. Such men, in attempting to teach, must evidently do more harm than good.

Anybody, therefore, who may be really anxious to acquire a good foundation in the art of swordsmanship, should be particular in the choice of an instructor.

In conclusion, since the habit of throwing forward the head and shoulders on the longe is condemned in these pages as the gravest fault a teacher can permit, the following extracts are cited from works of authority in support of the author's opinion. Many other works might be mentioned, but even from among those here noticed, the maxims of Gomard, Grisier, and Cordelois should be of themselves considered sufficient for the purpose:

Angelo, 1763.—"To Longe correctly, after the sword-hand has been advanced, all the other movements should follow rapidly, taking care *that the body be held erect and the head raised.*"

Demeuse, 1778.—"The frame, by being thrown forwards on the

longe, is cast off its balance, and placed in an inconvenient position. Through exhaustion, while in this posture it sinks beneath its weight. The fencer cannot recover without difficulty, and then only by several efforts. Moreover, his thoughts become confused, and with his arm restricted in action, he is unable to protect himself during the disorder of recovery."

La Boessierre, 1818.—In regulating the pupil's longe—"if the bust fall forward, it should be raised until *the erect position* is regained."

Roland, 1837.—In the longe "the left hip should be forced sufficiently home towards your right that the *body be quite erect* resting equally on both legs."

Gomard, 1845.—"Leaning forward on the longe should be avoided; for in doing so, with a view to increase the extension of the development, the recovery is rendered difficult; even more so than by overstriding."

"Young fencing-masters, credit my old experience, insist, at any sacrifice, upon your pupils employing the action of the fingers in handling the grip;—upon that action, together with the support of the frame in an erect position, success depends. Without the observance of these points, there can be no regularity; and without regularity, no good fencing."

"As in the position of defence, so also in the development of the longe, the body should be held *erect*, above the hips."

Grisier, 1847.—"The support of the body in an erect position is one of the most necessary points in Fencing. Through the observance of this principle the attack or return attack is rendered exact in its effect. The task of any teacher who endeavours to inculcate this excellent principle is always tedious; to check the natural tendency of leaning forward is contrary to our habits. We recommend all fencers to practise this restraint with the utmost perseverance. Upon it depends—success in loose play, or safety in serious combat."

"The pupil's body should be *kept in a perpendicular line* both in the defence and in the attack, for to allow the frame to fall forward is *defective in principle*."

Robalia, 1855.—"Upon the termination of the development of the longe the bust should be *upright*, without which there would be a difficulty in recovering."

Cordelois, 1862.—"I cannot admit that in any attack the body should be thrown forward.—This position is dangerous, useless as a means of reaching the opponent, and unfavourable towards the recovery from the right foot, after the attack."

"In the development of the longe the body should be throughout *steady* and *erect*."

www.ingramcontent.com/pod-product-compliance
Lightning Source LLC
Chambersburg PA
CBHW021109090426
42738CB00006B/563